THE AMERICAN EXPLORATION AND TRAVEL SERIES

EXPLORING THE NORTHWEST TERRITORY

Exploring the
NORTHWEST TERRITORY

SIR ALEXANDER MACKENZIE'S JOURNAL
OF A VOYAGE BY BARK CANOE
FROM LAKE ATHABASCA TO THE PACIFIC OCEAN
IN THE SUMMER OF 1789

Edited by T. H. McDonald

UNIVERSITY OF OKLAHOMA PRESS
Norman

LIBRARY OF CONGRESS CATALOG CARD NUMBER: 66–22719

Copyright 1966 by the University of Oklahoma Press, Publishing Division of the University. Composed and printed at Norman, Oklahoma, U.S.A., by the University of Oklahoma Press. First edition.

To my wife, Mary, and my son, Pat,
WHO, IN A SEVENTEEN-FOOT CANOE, SO COURAGEOUSLY
HELPED ME RE-EXPLORE THE NORTHERN ROUTE
OF SIR ALEXANDER MACKENZIE, 1789.

Acknowledgments

IT IS VERY DIFFICULT TO EXPRESS the gratitude that a historian has for those self-sacrificing people who work so diligently in libraries and archives, but I would like to try here to express my sincere thanks for the help received from the British Museum, the Dominion Archives of Canada, the Library of Congress, and the library of McGill University. Special thanks go to Miss Francine Morris of inter-library loan at Arlington State College for her patient work in collecting the leading secondary sources for my use. Miss A. M. Johnson, of The Hudson's Bay Record Society's archives at Beaver House, London, Mr. C. W. Kellaway of the Institute of Historical Research of the University of London, and Mr. Jean-Jacques Lefebvre, chief archivist of Superior Court, Montreal, gave me inestimable help. Then there were the men of the Hudson's Bay Company, the Northwest Territorial government, and the Royal Canadian Mounted Police who assisted us in our canoe journey. Finally, I must mention three dear friends: Dr. Charles Henner, who made up our medical kit for the journey, Angus Sherwood of Norman Wells, Northwest Territories, who straightened me out on a few things in the French-Canadian north, and last but far from least Miss Elizabeth Segerstrom, who found at the University of Washington and Washington State University the information that actually started me out on this task.

Arlington, Texas   T. H. McDONALD
July 28, 1966

Contents

Acknowledgments   *page* ix

Editor's Introduction   3

Mackenzie's Journal   25

    I. June 1789   25

    II. July 1789   45

    III. August 1789   94

    IV. September 1789   113

Addenda   119

   Letter from Dorchester to the Duke of Portland   119

   Letter from Mackenzie to Dorchester   119

Bibliography   122

Index   127

Illustrations

1. Portrait of Sir Alexander Mackenzie   *following page* 50
2. Ice packs on the Athabasca River
3. Harbor of New Fort Chipewyan
4. Entrance to the Rochers River
5. Rapids on the Slave River
6. Log jam on the Slave River
7. Mountain portage
8. Entrance to Great Slave Lake from the Jean River

9. View from the top of Granite Hill   *following page* 82
10. Great Slave Lake seen from the north channel of the Mackenzie River
11. "High hill" on the Mackenzie
12. Entrance of Great Bear River
13. Ramparts on the Mackenzie
14. Bear swimming in the Lower Ramparts
15. Mary and Pat near the Arctic Circle
16. The Mackenzie delta

MAPS

1. Mackenzie's route in 1789   *page* 20–21
2. Mackenzie's 1789 journey   37

EXPLORING THE NORTHWEST TERRITORY

Editor's Introduction

SIR ALEXANDER MACKENZIE, young director of the Athabasca district of the North West Fur Company, hardly an experienced explorer after one year at his post, left Old Fort Chipewyan on Lake Athabasca at nine o'clock in the morning, June 3, 1789. On July 12, at five o'clock in the evening, he reached Whale Island, in the Arctic Ocean, the most northerly point of his journey. Here "we were stopped by the Ice ahead and the shallowness of the water along shore, and we landed at the limit of our Travels in this Direction."[1] Thus ended the white man's last attempt to discover a Northwest passage around or through America. Mackenzie turned his back on the eternal ice packs of the Arctic Ocean to retrace his steps to Old Fort Chipewyan, where he arrived on September 12, 1789, at three o'clock in the afternoon. He felt that his expedition was a failure, not realizing that he had discovered one of the greatest water systems in the world: a water system that drains land equal in area to the Louisiana Purchase. In the annals of exploration this discovery stands out as one of the most significant, the more so because Mackenzie was a cartographer of surpassing excellence.

The published record of Mackenzie's journal of that epochal year was issued in December, 1801, in London and Edinburgh, under the title, *Voyages from Montreal on the River St. Laurence through the Continent of North America to the Frozen and Pacific Oceans in the Years 1789 and 1793.* Grave doubts about the authenticity of this work have been expressed by many students of exploration although Mackenzie seems to have autographed a number of copies of the book. It appears, from the best evidence so far available, that the account published in 1801 was put together by

[1] Alexander Mackenzie, *Journal to the North and Northwest Coast of America,* 75.

3

one William Combe.[2] Thus Mackenzie apparently took a course not uncommon in his time (or in ours), of putting notes, journals, and other papers in the hands of a professional editor. The fact that Combe was behind prison bars in 1801 does not necessarily indicate a lack of conscientious devotion on his part. But the discrepancies in the text of the book published in 1801 and the manuscript journal which Mackenzie presented to George Grenville, first Marquis of Buckingham, and which was bought by the British Museum in 1883, make it important that at long last the general public should have access to Mackenzie's own version.

The British Museum manuscript is written in at least three different hands. One of these is definitely that of Sir Alexander Mackenzie; of this there can be no doubt. The other two cannot be identified. It appears that the manuscript was reworked by Mackenzie in the winter of 1793–94.[3] Several pages also bear evidence that some recopying and changing was done; moreover, the Journal was bound after it was reworked.

This edition of the Journal has been taken directly from an accurate transcription of the manuscript in the British Museum. Since, however, it is not a facsimile, the editor has taken certain minor liberties with mechanical style in the interest of clarity and ease of reading. The method of dating entries has been made consistent throughout the Journal. Superior letters and figures have been brought down to align with other letters and a period used after abbreviations originally employing these raised letters. Occasionally, missing punctuation has been supplied or superfluous, confusing punctuation deleted.

---

[2] See Franz Montgomery, "Alexander Mackenzie's Literary Assistants," *Canadian Historical Review*, Vol. XVIII (1937), 301–304. The *Dictionary of National Biography* and the British Museum concur with the idea that William Combe was the compiler of the 1801 edition of *Voyages*. The Library of Congress does not express an opinion but quotes the above authorities.

[3] See Sir Alexander Mackenzie's letter to Roderick Mackenzie dated at Fort Chipewyan, March 5, 1794, and found in the L. R. Masson collection kept in the Public Archives of Canada, in Ottawa. In this letter he mentions to Roderick that he is copying his journal, having trouble doing it, and is expecting it to be finished by spring for Roderick's perusal.

Throughout the text, annotations point out variations between the Journal and the published book and delineate the sections that appear to have been reworked.

The common spelling of "Mackenzie" with a lower-case *k*, which is used by most modern historians, has been chosen for this edition even though existing copies of Mackenzie's signature indicate that he used a capital *K* slightly more often.

The historical importance of Mackenzie's 1789 voyage of discovery cannot be overemphasized: Until his exploration, very little was known by Europeans of the vast area north and west of Lake Athabasca.

The first information from white men concerning the great river and lake system of the far Northwest known today as the Mackenzie River System seems to have come to England in December, 1665, by means of a report probably given by George Carr to the Earl of Arlington, prominent member of the powerful Cabal under King Charles II:

> Hearing also some Frenchmen discourse in New England of a passage from the West Sea to the South Sea, and a great trade of beaver in that passage, and afterwards meeting with sufficient proof of the truth of what they had said, and knowing what great endeavours have been made for the finding out of a North-west passage, he thought them the best present he could possible make His Majesty, and persuaded them to come to England.[4]

Thus arrived Médard Chouart, sieur des Groseilliers, and his brother-in-law, Pierre Esprit Radisson, in London in the plague year. Here were two of the greatest of the great French-Canadian *voyageurs—coureurs de bois*, if you wish. These men had spent their adult lives in the wilds of frontier America: on the Great Lakes, down the Mississippi, across the western plains, up the rivers between the Great Lakes and the Hudson Bay area. Moreover, Radisson had heard from the Indians of the bay area of

[4] E. E. Rich, *The History of the Hudson's Bay Company, 1670–1870*, I, 23–24.

5

"another great lake leagues to the north whose upper end was always frozen." Some historians have taken this statement to refer to one or several of the lakes in the present Mackenzie River Basin.[5] Unfortunately, neither Radisson nor the Hudson's Bay Company records of this time say any more about this lake.

In 1670, Charles II gave control of all trade and government in the Hudson Bay area to the corporation known as the Hudson's Bay Company, whose authority remained unchallenged until the late eighteenth century. At that time rivals of the Bay Company formed the North West Company, which eventually became an important competitor. Naturally, most early exploration was directed by the powerful Hudson's Bay Company.

Bay Company records reveal that in the years 1715–16, William Stewart was sent out by James Knight, director at York Factory, to explore north and west, through the "Barren Desarts" to "the good country east of Slave River and south of Great Slave Lake." The apparent objective of this expedition—to put the Hudson's Bay Company in touch with the Great Slave Lake area—was accomplished, for as early as 1715 trade was opened between the Company and Athabasca, the Cree Indians being the middlemen. No white men were involved at the western end.[6]

Next, the great French explorer Pierre Gaultier de Varennes, sieur de la Vérendrye, and his followers pushed across the great western prairies in the 1740's to within sight of what some historians believe were the Rocky Mountains. The common opinion, however, is that neither he nor his followers ever went north of the Saskatchewan River.[7] Thus, they would not have come in contact with the great Mackenzie watershed since they did not cross the divide where the water begins to flow in a northerly direction. Actually the Hudson's Bay Company claims that their man, Anthony Henday, was in 1754 "the first white man to see the

[5] See A. C. Laut, *Pathfinders of the West*, 129.

[6] For further details of this early trade and the expedition of William Stewart see Rich, *History of the Bay Co.*, 434–36.

[7] See George Bryce, *Mackenzie, Selkirk, Simpson*, 3.

Rockies and the first to reach the Blackfoot Indians."[8] Be that as it may, he, like La Vérendrye, did not go north of the Saskatchewan River.

The role of William Grover in the history of northwestern exploration is somewhat debatable. Ferdinand Jacobs, Hudson's Bay commander at Churchill, proposed to send Grover into the Lake Athabasca region in 1759. Unfortunately, no report of the proposed journey seems to have survived in the records of the Hudson Bay Record Society.

During the 1760's the Hudson's Bay Company sent many men inland. Accurate or detailed accounts of their journeys are missing. We know that by 1766 these men were following the Saskatchewan River deep into the continent; by that date some had even reached the Red Deer River in present-day Alberta. It appears that the Company had been satisfied to remain contentedly on the bay until 1763, when the French and Canadian "Pedlars" (in Bay Company language, any non-Company trader) started pushing inland, intercepting the Indians who were on their way to trade with the Company. The year 1768–69 saw the Indians plunder the Pedlars' canoes and continue on to the bay for trading.[9] In 1766, three Dogrib Indians came in to trade at Churchill; known as the "Far Indians," they had never seen a post before. The Chipewyans acted as middlemen.[10] These Dogrib Indians, along with the Slave Indians, were the first Indians whom Mackenzie met on his journey

[8] This quotation has a most fascinating background. While wandering through a vacated trapper's cabin on the banks of the Mackenzie River within the Arctic circle, I came across an old Hudson's Bay calendar. All the months had been torn off; even the year of the calendar I do not know. But below the picture of Anthony Henday was a brief historical sketch of his 1754 expedition, written by Franklin Arbuckle, R.C.A. The above quotation is taken from this calendar, which is presently hanging in my office. A more lengthy discussion of Henday's journey can be found in Rich, *History of the Bay Co.*, 234–36. Rich does not, however, make the same claims for Henday that are found in Arbuckle's sketch.

[9] For this early rivalry for the trade of the Indians in the 1760's see Rich, *History of the Bay Co.*, II, 16–26. At no place, however, does it suggest that any white man actually journeyed north of the Saskatchewan River and into the Athabasca area.

[10] *Ibid.*, 47.

down the Mackenzie River.[11] Their home area lay between Great
Slave and Great Bear lakes.

According to an official release of the Department of Mines of
Canada, the "earliest explorations in the basin of the Mackenzie"
were made by Samuel Hearne between 1770 and 1772.[12] The Hudson Bay Record Society fills in much more of the details. Moses
Norton was in command at Churchill (Fort Prince of Wales) from
1762–73. He seems to have gotten into the good graces of Matonabbee, famous Indian leader of the Chipewyans[13] who had explored
much of the area between Lake Athabasca and Churchill prior
to 1768.[14]

It was from Churchill that Samuel Hearne set out on foot in
November, 1769, across the Barren Lands in search of the river
from which Indians obtained copper. Very early on this journey
his Indians deserted him and he was forced to return to Churchill.
He set off again in February, 1770, and was back at Churchill by
November 25, thanks only to Matonabbee, whom he had met out in
the Barrens. On his third attempt Hearne was willing to let Ma-
tonabbee make most of the arrangements. They left Churchill in
December, 1770,[15] reached the Coppermine River July 13, 1771,
and traveled home by way of Great Slave Lake and the Slave River.
They had evidently stayed in the rich country of the Slaves until
March of 1772,[16] for they did not reach Churchill until June 30.

[11] See MacKenzie's Journal entry for July 5, 1789.

[12] Charles Camsell and Wyatt Malcolm, "The Mackenzie River Basin," Canada
Geological Survey, Mus. Ball. No. 92 (1919), 2.

[13] Matonabbee is often known as "Chief of the Chipewyans at Fort Prince of
Wales." See Laut, *Pathfinders*, 249. It was owing to Matonabbee, supposedly, that
Norton carried on his lucrative fur trade with the other Indians of the Athabasca
region.

[14] Rich, *History of the Bay Co.*, II, 48.

[15] *Ibid.*, 53. On this page I believe that Rich or the printers have slipped on the
date used. At the bottom of the page Rich says that Hearne left for his third attempt
in December, 1772. Yet on page 58 Rich has Hearne's Journal in the hands of the
London committee in the "fall of 1772." To have completed his journey by 1772,
Hearne must have left in December, 1770.

[16] The dates which I have used for Hearne's three attempts are those used by
Rich (*History of the Bay Co.*, II, 49–56), with the exception of the corrections men-
tioned in footnote 15 above. There is no considerable disagreement between him and
Laut, who says that Hearne reached the mouth of the Coppermine River "July 17,

Although Hearne had been into the rich fur land of the Athabasca Indians or at least had skirted it, the Bay Company's London committee was far more interested in the area of the upper Saskatchewan River; their instructions in 1773 were for Ferdinand Jacob, commander at Fort York, "to establish a trading house inland as far up as the Pas or thereabouts" because of Pedlars intercepting Indians. Samuel Hearne was put in charge of establishing such a house.[17]

Thomas and Joseph Frobisher, from Montreal, had built a traders' fort at Sturgeon Lake on the Saskatchewan River as early as 1772.[18] In June, 1774, Hearne left for the interior. Clearing a site at Pine Island Lake, some sixty miles above Pas, he laid the origins of Cumberland House on September 3, 1774.[19] Thus began the rivalry for furs in the Northwest that was to rage for half a century, dyeing red the snows of Athabasca, the banks of the Saskatchewan, the rocky littoral of Superior, and the prairies of the Red River area.

On October 26, 1775, Peter Pond first reached Cumberland House along with Alexander Henry the elder, Joseph and Thomas Frobisher, and Charles Patterson. Mathew Cocking, of the Hudson's Bay Company, treated them civilly but as unwelcome guests since they were looked upon as Pedlars. They are said to have split and gone their several ways. There seems to have been no lasting alliance between these men; however, there is a suggestion that George Macbeath was backing Pond and that there was some combination behind Macbeath.[20]

1771" (*Pathfinders*, 265). Camsell and Malcolm (*Mackenzie Basin*, 2) have Hearne back at Churchill from his great discovery in June of 1772. There is some question also concerning the route he took on his return journey to Churchill. There seems to be no question that he was the first white man on Great Slave Lake and on Slave River, but a problem arises when one tries to ascertain where he left the Slave River and if he actually touched on Lake Athabasca, as there is a slight hint that he could have done. See Laut, *Pathfinders*, 269.

[17] Rich, *History of the Bay Co.*, II, 41–44.

[18] See Bryce, *Mackenzie, Selkirk, Simpson*, 4.

[19] Rich, *History of the Bay Co.*, II, 64–65.

[20] For possible alliances or combinations in the years 1775–76, see Rich, *History of the Bay Co.*, II, 67–69.

The summer of 1776 saw Thomas Frobisher, Joseph Frobisher, and the younger Alexander Henry meeting the Chipewyan Indians at Île à la Crosse. "The natives came from a country that had not yet been entered by any white man." From them Henry learned of the Peace River, Slave River, and Slave Lake.[21] This is the year that the name North West Company began to be used, but what or whom it denoted is not quite clear.

Louis Primeau brought Athabasca Indians from Île à la Crosse down to trade with the Bay Company in 1777. Shortly after this visit, Humphrey Marten, chief at Fort York, ordered an outpost to be built inland from Cumberland House, for that year, 1777–78, the Pedlars had surrounded Cumberland. They were organizing or organized, but apparently not along very strict lines. Although orders had also been given by the Bay Company for a new outpost, no attempt was made to build that year.[22]

Besides the items of interest mentioned above, the year 1777–78 holds a number of unresolved problems for the student of northwestern exploration, chief among them the question of who was the first white man to reach the Arctic watershed. Throughout the years historians have made various claims and advanced a number of hypotheses.

Arthur P. Woollacott, in *Mackenzie and His Voyageurs*, maintains that Peter Pond "was the first white man to cross over from the drainage basin of the Churchill to the Arctic watershed." He gives the year as 1778.[23] E. E. Rich, on the other hand, in his *History of the Hudson's Bay Company*, says that Charles Isham spent the winter of 1777–78 on "Beaver Lake and Athabasca . . . tenting near the Pedlar's post."[24] Thus it would seem that not one white

[21] Arthur P. Woollacott, *Mackenzie and His Voyageurs by Canoe to the Arctic and the Pacific, 1789–93*, 11–12. Bryce, *Mackenzie, Selkirk, Simpson*, 5, speaks of "Frobisher's men" penetrating to Lake Athabasca but does not say which ones or what years. The setting, however, would suggest 1776. More will be said shortly about the first white man to see Lake Athabasca.

[22] Rich, *History of the Bay Co.*, II, 72–75.

[23] Woollacott, *Mackenzie and His Voyageurs*, 13–14. With so many fur traders moving in this area I cannot see how Woollacott can be so certain.

[24] Rich, *History of the Bay Co.*, II, 75.

man but several had been on the Arctic watershed before Mackenzie. And since Beaver Lake is the westernmost part of the Churchill drainage basin, Isham rather than Pond was the first white man in this area.

There appears to be no doubt that Peter Pond was on the Athabasca River in 1778. Historians generally have accepted that fact. Charles Camsell and Wyatt Malcolm wrote:

> The first white man to appear on the Athabasca river was Peter Pond. . . . In 1778 he descended the Athabasca and founded a fort known as the "Old Establishment" about 30 miles above its mouth. He was also, evidently, the first white man to reach the shores of Lake Athabasca.[25]

Rich suggests that Pond went into the Athabasca country so far (to within thirty miles of Lake Athabasca) that he did not get out until July, 1779, in which month he arrived at Cumberland House.[26] Woolacott also points out that Pond built the "Old Establishment," which became his headquarters for the next six years, and adds that "it is generally accepted that Pond was the first white man to stand on the shores of Athabasca Lake."[27] Hume Wrong is not quite so specific; he states merely that Peter Pond was the "first white man to enter the Athabasca region."[28]

During 1779–82 both the Pedlars and the Bay Company men pushed ever north and west into the interior. The North West Company or Society was definitely formed in 1779, in sixteen shares, only to be dissolved at the end of the year. A new agreement was reached in 1780–81 among the opposition to the Bay

[25] Camsell and Malcolm, *Mackenzie Basin*, 2. I do not profess to know who got to the Athabasca River first among the many white fur traders. The three excellent sources cited here do not entirely agree. In regard to Pond's being the first white man on Lake Athabasca, Woollacott uses the term "generally accepted" and Camsell and Malcolm use "evidently." It would seem wise for writers to refrain from making dogmatic statements on the subject especially when we consider how many men were really active in these areas. My findings suggest that there are others who could have found their way into the Athabasca country before 1778 and who could perhaps have been the first there.

[26] Rich, *History of the Bay Co.*, II, 116.

[27] Woollacott, *Mackenzie and his Voyageurs*, 15–16

[28] Hume Wrong, *Sir Alexander MacKenzie*, 20.

Company, again in sixteen shares. The year 1778–79 brought the death of two white men as a result of difficulty between the Canadians and the Indians. During that same general period, 1779–80, a new Bay Company house was established farther inland and named Hudson's House. Peter Pond went back into the Athabasca country in 1780 and again in 1781–82. This latter year he was representing the great Canadian fur houses as opposed to Jean Étienne Waden, who was also in the northern regions representing the smaller houses. Waden was killed in the spring of 1782, at his post on Lac la Ronge. Evidence seemed to point to Pond as the killer, but he was acquitted.[29]

Near the beginning of 1782, this feverish activity of the Company and the Independents (Pedlars) in the Northwest was momentarily halted, or at least drastically curbed by events completely beyond the control of either faction. An epidemic of the dread disease smallpox broke out on the upper Saskatchewan in 1781–82, decimating the Indian population and bringing general disorder to the fur trade. Whites were not entirely immune to this crippling attack, especially if they had Indian blood. In addition to internal misfortunes, 1782 saw Hearne surrender Fort Churchill to the French and Fort York bow before the naval power of La Pérouse.

While the Hudson's Bay Company was busy recovering from the French invasion of 1782, the Independents were strengthening their position. In 1783–84 the North West Company was formally established,[30] the leading spirits being the brothers Frobisher and Simon McTavish. Unfortunately for the life of at least one man,[31] the latter association found no room for a rival merchant outfitter and buyer of furs which appeared in 1783 as Gregory, McLeod and

[29] For the activities of the years 1779–82 see Rich, *History of the Bay Co.*, II, 116–18.

[30] *Ibid.*, 118, uses the date of 1783–84. *The Encyclopedia Americana*, (1945 edition) XX, 431, agrees; however, the later date of 1787, when Gregory, McLeod and Company merged with the North West Company, is sometimes taken as the actual date for the organization of the true North West Company. See Bryce, *Mackenzie, Selkirk, Simpson*, or *The Columbia Viking Desk Encyclopedia* (1953 edition, II), 904.

[31] John Ross, of whom more will be said later.

Company.[32] The two Americans, Peter Pond and Peter Pangman, also stayed out of the North West Company, throwing in their lot with the smaller company for one season. But, in 1785, Pond became a partner in the North West Company.

Early in 1785, Pond returned to Athabasca as the representative of his company.[33] The following year he was responsible for setting up "Fort Resolution" on Great Slave Lake and for a visit farther north on the same lake to a point later called Fort Providence.[34] In writing about Pond's 1786 expedition, Woollacott mentions a possibility that could upset all the popular theories about the first white man or men in the Great Slave–Athabasca region. There is "a probability," he says, "that the French had been as far as Great Slave Lake before this, but whether before or after Hearne passed that way is not certain." As evidence he cites the report that "when the North-West Company reached it [Slave Lake] in 1786, they found there a family of French-Indian descent of the name of Beaulieu."[35]

In addition to Pond, representing the North West Company in

[32] A partnership of James Finlay and John Gregory dates back to 1773, but in 1783 Finlay retired and Norman McLeod took his place in the partnership. See Rich, *History of the Bay Co.*, II, 119–20.

[33] Rich, *History of the Bay Co.*, II, 120, suggests that Pond had already been to Lake Athabasca by himself and was returning with the idea of exploring the region between Lake Athabasca and the North Pacific Ocean.

[34] *Ibid.*, 120. Here we run into date and fact discrepancies. All sources seem to be agreed that Pond sent Cuthbert Grant and Laurent Leroux to establish a post on Great Slave Lake. Woollacott, *Mackenzie and his Voyageurs*, 16, places this event in 1788, which would seem to be definitely wrong, for by that date Pond was out of the Athabasca region and Alexander Mackenzie had taken it over. Furthermore, most of the other sources I have seen suggest or state that the year was 1786. That the post was known this early as Fort Resolution or any other fort is questionable. Mackenzie, when he arrived at this establishment in 1789, made this entry in his Journal for "Tuesday 9th" of June, 1789: "We steered East on the Inside of a long Sand Bank . . . till opposite the Houses which Messrs. Grant and Leroux built here fall 86." *Voyages* uses the fall of 1785. About the visit farther north little is written. But Mackenzie's entry of "Tuesday 23d" of June, 1789, definitely states that the "Red knife Indians," whom they met well above present-day Yellowknife Bay on the North Arm of Great Slave Lake, "had given parole [the promise of faith or friendship] to Mr. Leroux." Thus Mackenzie confirms the theory that Leroux had been in the Fort Providence area sometime before 1789.

[35] Woollacott, *Mackenzie and His Voyageurs*, 16.

the Athabasca region during the fur season of 1786–87, John Ross was there as a representative of Gregory, McLeod and Company. The details of what transpired between these two competitors are not clear, but the end result is well known. John Ross was killed, and the blame was laid on Pond. This second death within the same region in such a short period brought the merchants of Montreal to their senses. The North West Company was once more reorganized, in 1787, and Gregory, McLeod and Company was included in the new company, which took the name of the larger concern.[36]

The new North West Company was now looking for a strong man to take over the rich, unsettled Athabasca District. Such an individual was found in the youthful but courageous and vigorous Alexander Mackenzie.[37] This energetic young Scotsman had been with the fur merchants of Montreal some eight years. Prior to the merger of 1787 he had worked for Gregory, McLeod and Company, becoming a junior member of that organization sometime before the spring of 1785, the year he first journeyed into Indian country. At the company meeting in Grand Portage that year, he was appointed head of the Churchill River District. By that time Roderick Mackenzie, Alexander's cousin, had also joined Gregory, McLeod and Company and was at Grand Portage as apprentice clerk. After the two companies merged in 1787, Mackenzie was a shareholder as well as the new appointee to the Athabasca post, where he arrived on October 21, 1787.

[36] There is general agreement among leading authorities on the amalgamation of 1787. Of the murder of John Ross there seems to have been no definite proof. Pond went free, but soon was replaced and removed from the Athabascan area.

[37] Much has been written about the early life of Alexander Mackenzie, and many conflicting opinions expressed. In the ninth edition of the *Encyclopaedia Britannica*, published in 1883, an unlisted authority stated that Mackenzie was born in Inverness, Scotland in 1755. Adrian MacDonald, in *Canadian Portraits*, 15, agrees with this birth date. This would have made him thirty-two years old when he arrived on the Athabasca River. The 1960 edition of the *Britannica* retains this birth date. But in the 1960 edition of the *Encyclopedia Americana*, Mackenzie's birth date is given not as 1755, but 1764, and the place as the Hebrides rather than Inverness. The *Americana* date makes him a youth of twenty-three in 1787. M. S. Wade, one of the foremost biographers of Mackenzie, in his work *Mackenzie of Canada*, 18, places Mackenzie's birth at Stornoway, capital of the island of Lewis, largest of the Hebrides group, in the year 1763 or 1764.

That first winter in the Northwest with Peter Pond[38] was sufficient to set Mackenzie's imagination on fire. We have already seen
that Pond had proposed to find a route to the North Pacific from
Athabasca as early as 1785.[39] Now Mackenzie, building on the reports of the Indians concerning a great river leading west from
Great Slave Lake,[40] had visions of the long-sought and hoped-for
Northwest Passage. All he had to do was to discover it.

But first he needed a man whom he could trust to leave at the
fort. He therefore had his kinsman, Roderick Mackenzie, trans-
ferred into his district. Roderick's job was to move the "Old Establishment" from the river to Lake Athabasca. This he did, building
the new fort on a point of land on the southern shore of the lake
seven or eight miles east of the mouth of the river. They called it
"Fort Chepwean." (Today it is spelled Chipewyan; but many of
the Indians retain the old pronunciation.) They moved into the
new fort sometime before Christmas, 1788.

In this connection George Bryce relates a story which I have
been unable to find recorded in any other source. After stating that
Leroux and his party had been on Great Slave Lake considerably
before 1789, which seems to be common knowledge, he reports that
Mackenzie sent Leroux back to Slave Lake another time. According to Bryce, Leroux took "English Chief," a Chipewyan leader,
with him. They advanced beyond Slave Lake, and Leroux sent a
sturdy Highland trader named Sutherland "to visit distant tribes
of Indians and win their good-will by a liberal distribution of presents." That Sutherland was successful is implied by the fact that
the following spring a large number of Indians from a lake far to
the west came to Leroux with furs. Unfortunately Bryce does not
name the lake far to the west nor does he give any dates except to
indicate that the journey was made before 1789.[41]

Whatever Leroux did, the spring of 1789 found Alexander Mac-

---

[38] Pond left Athabasca in 1788 never to return. See Rich, *History of the Bay Co.,*
II, 135.
[39] See footnote 33 above.
[40] Bryce, *Mackenzie, Selkirk, Simpson,* 30.
[41] *Ibid.,* 18.

kenzie ready and eager to be off on his quest for the great river that flowed out of the west end of Great Slave Lake. The question now arises, was he the first white man on this river which today bears his name? Bryce's account of Leroux's activities makes one wonder, although all the other historians I have consulted do not question that Mackenzie was the first white man on the river that drains Great Slave Lake. Indeed, while Leslie Roberts, in his comparatively recent work, *The Mackenzie*, gives Hearne and others the credit of being the first in that vast area north and east of Great Slave Lake, he yet declares that it was Mackenzie who first swung west.[42]

Perhaps it would be better to let Mackenzie's Journal speak for itself regarding what the Indians on that great river knew about white men when Mackenzie found them. The explorer entered the river from Deep Bay through the North Channel on June 29, 1789. He did not see his first river Indians until July 5, after he had traveled some 470 or 480 miles downstream. His Journal entry for that day states that there were "26 or 30 Persons"; further, that "it was evident they did not know the use of Tobacco," their clothing was made of "Skin," their "Bracelets, gorgets, Arm & wrist Bands . . . of wood, Horn or Bone," and their "Dishes of Wood, Bark or horn"—none of which suggest contact with the white man. Perhaps the primary evidence that they had not come into contact with any European or Asian is their almost complete lack of metal. Mackenzie was struck by the way they cooked their food which he explains in detail:

> . . . the Vessel which serve them to cook their Victuals are something of the shape. of a Gourd wide & bilged below & narrower at top make of Wallup Basket work, but so close that it holds Water with any other thing they chuse to put in it, They make it boil by putting a sufficiency of Red hot Stones into it. those Vessels contain from 2 to 6 gals.

He goes on to describe their making of thread by working "Bark . . . upon their Thigh." They make their "Lines of the Sineues of

[42] Leslie Roberts, *The Mackenzie*, 30.

Rein Deer, their Hooks of Wood, Horn, or Bone, their arms . . . are Bows & Arrows, Spears, Daggs, & pogmagans." The only inkling that these Indians had ever come in contact with products of the white man's world is in the description of the "Arrows" that were "2½ ft. long including the Point which is of bone, Horn, Stone Iron or Copper." Their axes were made of "brown or grey Stone . . . they made Fire by striking together a piece of White or Yellow Pirclis & a Flint Stone."

Now, the question is, where did they get the iron and copper? Although they seemed to have very little of these metals, they did have some. The same question must have bothered Mackenzie, for the Journal provides an answer. (It must be remembered that at no time did Mackenzie find Indians on the great river with whom his Indians could not communicate. At times, it is true, communication was slow and awkward, but it was always possible.) Thus the Journal states for that same day, July 5:

> . . . they have small bits of Iron which they get from the next Tribe to them, those from the Red Knives & Chippiweans in barter for Martin Skins & a few Beaver—they make knives of those small bits of Iron by fixing them in the End of a small Stick with those & Beaver Teeth they finish all their work.

Above and below what today is called the Ramparts and Fort Good Hope, Mackenzie found a goodly number of Indians. He likens them all to those mentioned earlier, so much so that he does not bother to describe their customs. Some of the Indians tried to run away, some did not; all responded favorably to gifts.

On "Thursday 9th" of July, Mackenzie first met some of the *"Diguthe Dinees"* or Quarreller Indians, perhaps thirty to forty miles downstream from present-day Little Chicago and some ninety to one hundred miles from the delta region of the great river. He found that their "arms and utensils" differed "but little from those I have already described." He did point out once again that "they have no Iron except very small Pieces that serve them for Knives, which they get from the Eskmeaux." Their cooking vessel was "of a thin frame of wood." Before leaving these Indians, the *Voyageurs* saluted them with "a Couple of guns load with Powder at the Report of which the Indians were startled, having never heard or seen anything of the kind before." In fact, it scared them so much that the new guide Mackenzie had hired from among them was ready to desert before he actually began. Mackenzie's own Indians had to make him understand "that what we had done was as a Sign of Friendship." A short distance downriver they came upon more of the same tribe on the same day and discovered that "They were fonder of Beads than anything else I gave particularly Blue ones, one of them to whom I had given a Knife asked me to change it for three Branches of Beads which I did."

Unfortunately, Mackenzie found no more Indians before reaching the delta and found no "Eskmeaux" in the delta or on the Arctic Ocean. He did find many of the "Eskmeaux" huts and camp grounds. Also on "Sunday 12th" of July he found "a square Stone Kettle, could contain about 2 galls. . . . wooden Dishes and Troughs." Even when on Friday, July 17, Mackenzie found "Sledges," he discovered that they were put together with "wooden Pegs Pieces of small Bone or Horn."

Once back into the river and among the Quarreller Indians, Mackenzie found that these natives put "little value" in iron and would rather have beads, for which they traded fish. Mackenzie, on his return trip—Wednesday, July 23—questioned these Indians extensively and learned that "the Eskmeaux saw large Canoes full of white men to the Westward 8 or 10 Winters since, from whom they got Iron of which they [the Indians] exchang'd part with them for leather." The place to which the big canoes came the "Eskmeaux" called *"Belan howlay Tock"* or "white Mens lake."

Back in the present-day Fort Good Hope area, Mackenzie, on Sunday, July 26, related that the Indians "were very fond of Iron work of any kind." These Indians told of another "large River on the other Side of the Mountains to the S. W. which falls into the *"Belhowlay Toe."* To the entrance of this river "Canoes say Ships" had come. Mackenzie encouraged the Indian, "Dog Rit," with whom he was talking, to get skins "to barter for Iron with his own Nation, who are now supplied with Goods by French People near their Land."

The following day, "Monday 27th," in the same general locality, Mackenzie learned of a "white mens Fort" about which these river Indians had been told. It was supposedly at the mouth of the great river on the west side of the mountains. Mackenzie felt that the Indians knew "more about the Country [that is, the area of the other great river] than they chuse to tell me at least than what comes to my Ears." Unfortunately, he had to rely on his own Indians to interpret. He well knew that his own Indians were tired and did not want to travel across a mountain and down another river and that the Indians who gave the information feared that one or more of their number might be forced to become a guide for this journey.

Mackenzie saw few and met fewer Indians from this point until he was once more on Great Slave Lake. It seems that the closer he got to the lake, the more fearful the Indians were of his presence. From the few he met, he could learn no more than he already knew of the other great river to the west, although each group of Indians to which he spoke seemingly knew by hearsay of the river. On "Thursday 13th" of August, his hunters' firing at geese scared a group of "Natives" so badly that Mackenzie never was able to catch them, though he tried to track them for some time. This incident took place not far from the mouth of the Liard River. Two days later the explorers found dwellings that made them think "some of the Red Knives must have come down this length . . . tho it is not customary."

Near present-day Fort Providence, some fifty or sixty miles downriver from Great Slave Lake, on "Thursday 20th." of August, Mackenzie "found a Paddle and an awl on the water side." He recognized the paddle as belonging to the "Crees," and the awl was, of course, a trade item of the white man. He felt it could have been a war party. Two days later he entered Great Slave Lake once more.

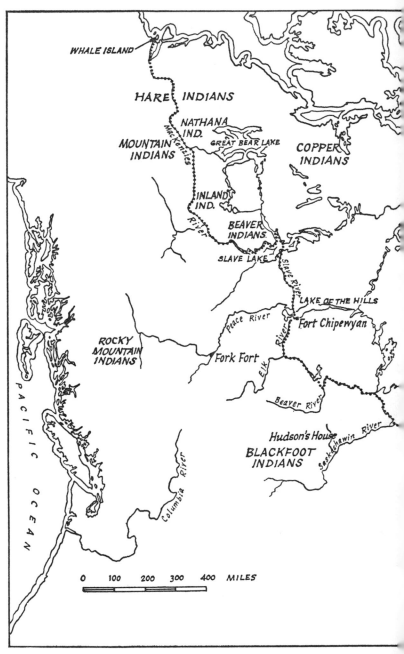

A MAP OF CANADA showing Mackenzie's route across Canada to his
on Lake Athabasca and his journey from the fort to the Arctic in 1

...ken from the 1801 edition of *Voyages*, with original spellings of ...ce names.

What, then, can we conclude from these descriptions of the Indians whom Mackenzie found on the great river which now bears his name, especially in respect to their knowledge of the white man and his contact with them? First, there seems to be no doubt that most or all of these river Indians knew of the white man. All or most of them had come into possession of his materials in the form of bits of iron. It is possible but not probable that some of those whom Mackenzie met had actually been into the area of Great Slave Lake to trade with the Frenchmen. Certainly we have reason to believe that some of the river Indians near Great Slave Lake knew much of the white man and had traded with him. These Indians Mackenzie never met, perhaps because of the war party of Crees. In his Journal entry for August 20, 1789, Mackenzie indicates that the river Indians were scared by the Crees. Nowhere, however, does he suggest that any white man before him had ever seen the Great Slave Lake outlet of the great river. Nor have I been able to discover any other evidence to indicate the white man's earlier presence. It is possible that some Frenchman, trapper, *coureur de bois*, or other rover could have entered the river, but until a definite record is brought to light, the discovery of the headwaters of the Mackenzie River by the white world will have to be attributed to Alexander Mackenzie.

Turning to the great delta region of the Mackenzie River, again we must rely on Mackenzie's Journal. That the "Eskmeaux" were acquainted with the white world and had traded with the white man cannot be denied. How far white traders had come toward the Mackenzie delta, we know not. Perhaps an ambitious Russian party had actually found the delta, although I know of no such claim. It is likely that the "Eskmeaux" of the Mackenzie delta had gone to the white man rather than that the white man had come to them. Mackenzie's record of the delta region remains the first record of this region known at present to the white world.

To follow Sir Alexander Mackenzie's course in the twentieth

century by the means he chose, namely canoe, is no easy task. But in 1965, using Mackenzie's manuscript as a guide, my wife Mary, my seventeen-year-old son Pat, and I experienced the most invigorating, back-breaking, breathtaking voyage of our lives. Our means was a seventeen-foot canoe, propelled by paddles, and our journey was from Old Fort Chipewyan to the Arctic Ocean. By this undertaking we hoped to give to the task of editing Mackenzie's journal of 1789 greater insight and an immediacy which can never be achieved solely from documents and books, no matter how great or reliable.

Mackenzie left Old Fort Chipewyan on June 3, 1789.[43] We left the same place on June 4, 1965. Mackenzie reached Great Slave Lake on June 9; we on June 20. He entered the north channel of the Mackenzie River on June 29, having taken twenty days to paddle across the lake, up the north arm, and down the north side into the river. We entered the north channel on July 8, having taken eighteen days to follow Mackenzie's tortuous route around Great Slave Lake. Mackenzie entered the Arctic Ocean on July 12, 1789, having run the Mackenzie River in thirteen days. We entered the ocean on August 3, 1965, having taken twenty-six days to paddle down the Mackenzie. Obviously Mackenzie's men were better paddlers than we.

Our rustic journey provided us with much excitement and pleasure, ranging from a water race with a bear and a storm with five-foot breakers on the lake to a blueberry feast only ten miles below the Arctic Circle. But of course the most important result of the trip, and its main objective, was for us to learn at first hand the hazards Mackenzie faced, the conditions under which he was traveling, and the precise distances and directions he traveled. Thus the annotations in this edition, in which I have tried to correct the discrepancies between the published 1801 version and the

---

[43] Even here many sources do not agree. MacDonald, *Portraits*, 18, has Mackenzie leaving Old Fort on June 5, 1789. The *Encyclopaedia Britannica*, 1883 edition, says he left July 3, 1789. Newer editions omit the date.

earlier unpublished one, reflect not only available documentary and published data, but information gained directly from personal experience as well.

As can be seen from my annotations, I frequently found the handwritten Journal to be more correct in its observations and directions than Combe's amended *Voyages*, a fact which provides a final important reason for the publication now of the long-ignored original Journal of 1789.

Mackenzie's Journal

JOURNAL OF A VOYAGE PERFORMED BY ORDER OF THE N.W. COM-
PANY, IN A BARK CANOE IN SEARCH OF A PASSAGE BY WATER
THROUGH THE N.W. CONTINENT OF AMERICA FROM ATHABASCA TO
THE PACIFIC OCEAN IN SUMMER 1789.

WEDNESDAY 3 June at 9 oclock embarked at Fort Chepwean, Mr. Leroux[1] with Canoe for Slave Lake in Company, Steered W. 21 Miles, then N.N. West 9 Miles when we entered the River, or one of the Branches or Outlets of this Lake, of which there are several. We steer North 6 Miles.[2] Then N.N.E. 2 Miles   Here we camp'd at 7 oclock P.M.   our Hunters kill'd a goose and pr. Ducks. One of the men [shot?] a Duck which he swam for, our Canoe being taken out of the water and the other men gumming her.

THURSDAY 4TH.—Embarked at 4 this morning and steered N.N.E. ½ miles N. 1½. N. 2 miles, then W.N. ½ mile N.N.W. ½ mile W.N.W. 2 miles,[3] here this Branch joins the Peace River being the lowest. Its very remarkable that in all those Branches the Current when the Peace River is high in May and August run into

[1] In the 1801 edition of *Voyages from Montreal on the River St. Laurence through the Continent of North America, to the Frozen and Pacific Oceans; in the Years 1789 and 1793*, this gentleman is "M. LeRoux, one of the Company's clerks." Future references to this formidable title will be abbreviated to *Voyages*.

[2] "North five miles," in *Voyages*.

[3] In *Voyages* these directions read: "North-North-East half a mile, North one mile and a half, West two miles, North-West two miles, West-North-West one mile and a half, North-North-West half a mile, and West-North-West two miles, when this branch loses itself in the Peace River." From "North-West two miles" to the end, these directions are completely off. Had we tried to follow them, we would have found ourselves carrying our canoe several miles through forested land. Although Mackenzie has his directions right in the main, he is short on the length of that "River" (the present-day Rocher River) at least five or six miles if not more, depending on which channel he took. This is typical of Mackenzie's reckoning. He is usually short, seldom long.

the Lake: from the Lake to this [blank space[4]] 200 yds wide nor their [less?] than 120, the Banks are low here and there, a Hugh Rock, the Lowland is well covered with wood, such as white Birch, spruce or Pine of difft. kind. Poplar, Willows of three kinds and asper Tree.[5] In this River[6] we find the Current stronger, its about a mile wide here, and its course N.W. 2 miles N.N.W. through Islands 6 miles, North 4½ miles N. b E. 2 miles W. b N. 6 miles N. 1 mile N.E. b E 2 miles N.N.W.[7] 1 mile, went down a rapid N.W. 7½ miles N.W. 9 miles N. b W. 6 miles, N.W. b W. 1½ mile North W. b N. ½ mile. N.N.W. 6 miles. N. 1 Mile. N.W. b W. 4 miles N.N.E. 1 mile, land, unload our Canoes at the Dog River (at half past Seven on the east side close by the Rapids, the Hunters killed 2 geese, and the men killed a goose and 2 Ducks. The River is near 2 Leagues wide here.

FRIDAY 5TH.—We embarked at 3 oclock this morning and unloaded our Canoe at this first rapid. here we enter a small River or channel which is occasioned by Islands   in half an hours time we came to the Carriens place   Its 300 paces long, and good except at the farther End, We had some Difficulty in loading there being a quantity of Ice not yet thawed, from this to the next are 6 miles[8]

---

[4] Here is a blank space in the Journal which Mackenzie seems never to have tried to fill. The next two lines do not make good sense. *Voyages* clears up the entire problem thus: "It is remarkable, that the currents of these various branches of the lake, when the Peace River is high, as in May and August, run into the Lake, which in the other months of the year returns its waters to them; whence to this place, the branch is not more than two hundred yards wide, nor less than an hundred and twenty. The banks are rather low, except in one place, where an hugh rock rises above them." This is an excellent example of Combe's filling in what he felt should be there. Unfortunately he is wrong concerning the width of the "branch," which actually is over half a mile wide in places. Also there are several places, not just one, where "an huge rock rises above" the banks.

[5] *Voyages* calls this asper tree a "liard."

[6] The "Slave River" in *Voyages*.

[7] In *Voyages* this direction is "North one mile." Mackenzie's calculations for this day are about ten miles off. He in fact traveled over eighty miles.

[8] The next few lines are not clear in meaning and there is some discrepancy with *Voyages*; thus I quote from that edition: "From hence to the next carrying place, called the *Portage d'Embarras*, is about six miles, and is occasioned by drift wood filling up the small channel, which is one thousand and twenty paces in length; from hence to the next is one mile and a half, while the distance to that which succeeds, does not exceed one hundred and fifty yards. It is about the same length as

Portage d Embarass occasioned by Drift wood[9] filling the small channel, its 1020 Paces long   from here to the next 1½ mile 350 Paces long, to the next not above 150 yds.[10] its about the same length from here to the Mountain about 4 miles and we enter the Grand River, this small River is by much the best Road there being no danger, tho' I believe a shorter road might be found upon the Outside of the Islands and not so many Carry Places   The Mountain is 335 Paces long, and from here to the Pelican Portage (820 Paces) about a Mile,[11] all dangerous Rapids, the landing is very steep and quite close to the fall, all Hands were for some time handing the loading and Canoe up the Hill, one of the Indian Canoes went down the Fall, but was lucky enough to jump out of her, she was broke to Pieces lost all her menage—From where we started this morning the Course is about N.W. and distance 15 miles from this to the next carrying Place is about 9 miles[12] 3 Rapids course N.W. b W. the Portage is very bad and 535 Paces long, our Canoes light passed on the Outside of an Island opposite,[13] made a portage of not more than the length of a Canoe—In rapids

the last; and from hence to the carrying place called the Mountain, is about four miles further; when we entered the great river." Notice that the Journal uses the term "Grand River" and gives a distance, "350 paces long," left out in *Voyages*.

[9] The driftwood was still there in 1965 when we made the portage. About half a mile of this small river is so closely packed with driftwood that one can walk with ease across the river.

[10] These latter two portages we made in one. In recent years very few people use these portages on the east side of the river. Only the old trappers and Indians risk this sixteen-mile stretch of white water. The Canadian government has built a highway from Fort Fitzgerald, one mile above the Dog River, to Fort Smith, just below the last rapids. All river cargo is transported over this highway by truck today.

[11] The Mountain and the Pelican portages we did in one by crossing to the west side of the "Grand River" and then recrossing through the "fast" water. The water is swift, the work hard, but it saves the last half-mile portage. The route we took is one the *voyageurs* discovered some years after Mackenzie's expedition. Two weeks before we crossed, two trappers almost drowned on this crossing when their canoe turned over.

[12] Here Mackenzie overestimates the distance, one of the few times he ever does. The main river bed from the Dog River to the last rapid is about sixteen miles. One should add, perhaps, three or four miles extra for the circuitous route taken by Mackenzie in following a side channel.

[13] By going on the inside of an island group, we missed all these latter rapids mentioned by Mackenzie and made one large portage of about one-quarter of a mile, after which we crossed the "Grand River" to Fort Smith.

upon the other side of the River there were 5 men drowned and 2 Canoes and some Ps.[14] lost going to the Slave Lake fall 86[15] under charge of Mr C Grant, from this we steered S.W. 6 miles and camped upon Point Du Roch half past 5 P.M. men and Indians very much fatigued, They killed a Beaver 7 Geese and 4 Ducks.

SATURDAY 6TH.—We embarked at ½ past 2 A.M. and steered N.W. b. N. 21 miles N.W. b W. 5 miles W.N.W. 4 miles W. 6 miles turned a point N.N.E. 1 mile E. 5 miles N.E. 1 E. 2 miles[16] N.W. b N. 1 ½ miles W.N.W. 3 miles N.E. b E. 2 miles, turn a point W 1 ½ mile[17] W. b N. 9 miles N.W. b W. 6 miles N.N.W. 5 miles, here we landed, unloaded and camped for the night at 6 oclock set a Net in a small River close by   Had a Head Wind the most part of the Day so cold that the Indians made use of their mittens. killed 7 geese and 6 Ducks.

SUNDAY 7TH.—We set off at ½ past 3 A.M. steered W.N.W. 1 mile round an Island C.[18] 1 mile N. b W.[19] 2½ miles S. b. W. 3 miles W.S.W. 1 mile S.W. b S. ½ mile N.W. 3 miles W.N.W. 3½ miles N. 7 ½ miles[20] being raining for some time it came on so hard that we were obliged to land and unload to prevent our goods getting wet, in an hours time it cleared up, and we reloaded and got underway, steered N. 10 miles W. 1½ mile N. 1½ mile, the rain came on again and obliged us to put in shore for the night,

[14] The Ps. is expanded to packages in *Voyages*.

[15] Expanded to "fall of 1786" in *Voyages*.

[16] In place of "N.E. 1 E. 2 miles," *Voyages* has just "North two miles."

[17] In place of "turn a point W 1½ mlie," *Voyages* reads "doubled a point one mile and a half"; no direction is given. Again Mackenzie is short on mileage. He did well over eighty miles this day.

[18] The "C." or anything it might stand for is left out in *Voyages*. It states merely, "round an island one mile."

[19] "North-West two miles and a half," in *Voyages*.

[20] *Voyages* adds "North-West by North four miles, North two miles and a half, North-West by North two miles." Why these extra directions and mileage were added is not at all clear, since the directions given in the Journal are in general correct, though not exact. (Mackenzie's mileage is again short.) The extra miles appear nowhere in Mackenzie's own version, and since it is very unlikely that Mackenzie would try to remember and correct these exact directions so long after he made the journey, they seem to be an error on the part of the editor who prepared *Voyages*. At the point where the added directions would start, the river flows northeast rather than northwest.

about ½ past 3 P.M. we had a strong N.N.E. wind all Day which hindered us much, Mr. Leroux's People passed not finding this Place agreeable, the men and Indians killed 2 geese and 2 Ducks, rained the rest of the Day

MONDAY 8TH.—It blew exceeding hard with rain all last night and this Day till 2 in the afternoon when the Rain subsided, but the wind unlimited which prevented our moving this Day.

TUESDAY 9TH.—We embarked at ½ past 2 A.M. calm and Foggy, soon after 2 young men joined us that we had not seen for 2 days, they killed 4 Beavers and 10 geese which they gave me—Our course N.W. b N. 1 mile. Opposite here is an opening in the right which we took for a Fork of the River but proved to be a Lake. We came back and steered S.W. b S.[21] 1½ miles W.S.W. 1½ miles W. 1 mile, here we entered a small River on the East side. They tell me that there used to be a carrying Place at the Entry owing to Drift Wood filling up the Passages, but the water has carried it away, the course of it is winding but suppose it will be about North distance 10 miles to where it falls into the Slave Lake,[22] and where we arrived at 9 A.M., we found a great change in the weather, it being excessive Cold. The Lake is covered all over with Ice and does not seem to have yet moved, excepting along the shore, all along the River we were much troubled with Muskettows and gnatts, but now I believe they must take their leave of us till the weather gets warmer—from below the Rapids (as well as above) upon either side the River the Banks are well covered with all the Kinds of wood peculiar to this country, particularly the West side, the land being lower and a richer soil (black Earth) on the East side, the Banks are high, the soil is yellow Clay and Sand, so that the wood is not so big nor so numerous, the ground is not yet thawed above 18[23] Inches deep, notwithstanding the Leaf is at its full growth, tho' there is hardly the appearance of any yet along the Lake—The Indians tell me that at a very little distance on both

---

[21] "South-West by West," in *Voyages*.

[22] Here Mackenzie's mileage is extremely short. This small river, the Jean River, is at least twenty-five miles in length.

[23] "14 Inches" rather than "18 Inches," in *Voyages*.

Sides the River are very extensive Plains, where there are vast Herds of Buffaloes, and that the Moose Deer[24] and the largest kind of Rain Deer keep in the Wood close by the River, the Beaver (which are numerous) build their Houses in small Lakes, and Rivers, which they cannot do in the larger River as the Ice carries every thing along with it   in the Spring all the Banks of the River are covered with Wild Fowl, We killed 2 swans 10 geese 1 Beaver this morning without losing an hour's time, so that if we were [here?] for the purpose of hunting we might soon fill our Canoe from the small River we steered East on the Inside of a long Sand Bank[25] (covered with Drift wood and a few Willows which reaches till opposite the Houses which Messrs. Grant and Leroux built here fall 86[26]   we ran aground often finding 3 feet water when deepest for 6[27] miles, and here we found Mr. Leroux who had arrived only in the Morning, had not seen him since the 7th., we unloaded our Canoe, and pitched our Tents, for from what we could see we would be obliged to remain here some time   I ordered the men to set Nets immediately as we could not touch our Provision during our stay at this place, which they soon did and caught plenty of Fish for our Supper Say Poisonenconu white Fish, Trout, Carp etc.[28]

WEDNESDAY 10TH.—Rained for the greatest part of the last night and this day till the afternoon, which has weakened the Ice

[24] "Moose" in *Voyages*; the deer is left off as is would be today.

[25] This sandbank must have become part of the mainland since 1789; no longer is there one running from the mouth of the Jean River to opposite Grant point. About halfway to Grant point there is such a sandbank that continues for several miles, and the last three or four miles also have a sandbank protecting an inner waterway.

[26] The fall of 1785, in *Voyages*.

[27] "5 miles," in *Voyages*. This "6 miles" is the only distance Mackenzie gives in discussing the distance from the mouth of the Jean River to Grant Point. The actual distance is near twenty miles. To get these distances absolutely correct is almost impossible because of the sandbars, driftwood, and rocks one must go around. Even the maps released by the Canadian government in recent years are not always exactly accurate.

[28] Mackenzie seems to have been unfamiliar with some of the fish he caught, and, if he meant "unknown fish" by his "poisonenconu," his French was not very good. In *Voyages* this passage reads:"The fish we now caught were carp, poisson inconnu, white fish, and trout."

much.   I sent 2 young men a Hunting to a River[29] 9 miles from here; where they tell me there used to be many animals, the Fishery not so good as yesterday

THURSDAY 11TH.—Strong westerly winds fine clear weather the women went to gather Berries, of which they brought us many (Say Cramberries) and are very plentiful in this country—went with one of the Men to a small Island close bye where we picked up some Dozens of Swan, geese and Duck Eggs, and killed a Brace of Ducks and a goose—upon my arrival I was informed that Mr. Leroux had a very serious dispute with his foreman, but as neither of the Parties made any Complaint, I did not think proper to take any notice of it.[30] In the Evening the young men returned without finding any large animals, they killed a swan and a grey Crain. Caught but 5 fish to day and only peik,[31] which People in this Country are not fond of, being too common, The Ice moved a little to the Eastward

FRIDAY 12TH.—The Weather as yesterday   towards noon our old Companions (the Muskettoes) visit us in greater numbers than we would wish as they are very troublesome guests, the Ice moved again in the same Direction, I ascended a Hill[32] close by, but could not perceive that the Ice had been broke in the middle of the Lake. Hunters killed a goose and 3 Ducks.

SATURDAY 13TH.—Cloudy Weather, the wind changeable   about Sun Set it settled in the N.E.[33] and drove back the Ice much broken along shore, and covered our Netts. One of the Hunters that had been at the Grand[34] River since last Night came back with 3

---

[29] "Lake" rather than "River," in *Voyages*. There are both small lakes and small rivers that would be within this distance. However, the larger Taltson River would seem to be the most reasonable objective. It is not much over nine miles from Grant Point.

[30] The lines telling of this dispute are left out of *Voyages*.

[31] Spelled "pike," in *Voyages*.

[32] Mackenzie fails to mention that all this area, including the hills, is solid rock. There are no buildings here today, but there are two small areas with a few trees and some shallow soil that could have been the location of the houses built by Grant and Leroux.

[33] "North," in *Voyages*.

[34] "Slave River," in *Voyages*.

Beavers and 14 geese, he was accompanied by 3 Families of Indians who had left Athabasca the same day that we did, they did not bring me a single Fowl, they said that they marched so hard, that they could not kill enough of Provision for their Families. By a Meridian line I found the variation of the Compass to be about 20 Degrees Easterly.

SUNDAY 14TH.—Clear Weather, wind as last Night, We run a risk of losing our Netts, as there is no getting at them, at sun set appearance of a violent gust of wind from the Southerd, the Sky in that quarter of a sudden became the blackest dark blue colour and lightened much, however it passed away without any wind, but came on very heavy Rain which inevitably must diminish the Ice in its present shattered Condition

MONDAY 15TH.—In the Morning the Bay still full of Ice And Can't get at our Netts. About Noon the wind veered to the Westerd and uncovered our Netts, and cleared a Passage to the opposite Islands, we raise our Netts very much broken and not many Fish. Struck our Tents loaded and embarked at Sun Set   made the Traverse in two Hours time, about 8 Miles N.E. b N.   unloaded upon a small Island and gummed our canoe at ½ past 11 P.M. being then as clear as to see to write this, we have not seen a star since the second Day we left Athabasca. About 12 o'clock the Moon made her appearance a little above the Top of the Trees, the under Horn eclipsed and continued so for about 6 minutes; not a cloud to be seen. I sounded three times in the Traverse, found 6 feet[35] water and a muddy Bottom.

TUESDAY 16TH.[36]—It blew very hard from the Northerd this

[35] In *Voyages*, "six fathoms water, with a muddy bottom." This would be between thirty and thirty-six feet, which is a large difference from the original. It is possible that the printer, wanting to use the right term, lost the true meaning, or perhaps he did not feel such a large lake could be so shallow. In crossing this same area, however, we sounded several times and the water ranged from three to ten feet deep. If there are much deeper spots, we never found them.

[36] In the Journal this number looks more like "10th," except that the "0" is not closed on the left side. It is possible that Mackenzie's pen slipped as it seemed to do often in his writing. After all, he was not writing under the most favorable circumstances. An open-air camp, a tent, or even a fort with candle or oil lamp does not provide the best conditions for a scribe.

morning which prevented our Embarking, a vast quantity of floating Ice   the Men and Indians caught some Trout with Hook and Line.   Set a Nett which we took up again at 12 with three small Fish. I had an observation which gave 61°–28 North. The wind moderated and we embarked about one our Course N.W. thro' Islands 10 Miles   we took in much Water making several Traverse at 5 P.M. we landed and Camped, set Netts and Hook and Lines. The Indians kill'd a goose. N. B. Thundered this Day.

WEDNESDAY 17TH.—Rose our Netts & caught but 17 Fish, stopp'd within a Mile of our Campment by the Ice. The Indians brought us back to a point where we made a very good Fishery, and they went a hunting as well as to look out a Passage amongst the Islands. At 3 P.M. they returned without meeting with any large animals, they could not observe any Passage, but we expect that the wind which blows strong from the N.E. will make a Passage. They killed two geese[37]—about sun set the weather became much overcast, Thunder, lightening and Rain.

THURSDAY 18TH.—At 4 this morning took up our Netts & with plenty of Fish, and we steered N.W. 4 miles, when the Ice again stopped us, the wind S.E. drove the Ice amongst the Islands right in our way, and we could perceive at some distance a Head that it was not much broken. Set our Netts & in 4 feet[38] water. Two of our Hunters killed a Rain Deer and young one, they had seen two Indians with their Families. One of the Indians came to see us about 7 o'clock. had nothing   they live upon Fish. they are waiting the Lake being clear to go to the other side of it—he says that the Ice has not yet stirred on the other side of a large Island opposite to us. No Fishery.[39]

FRIDAY 19TH.—This Morning visited our Netts and Caught but 6 Fish which are very bad   in the forenoon the Indians went a

[37] "They killed two geese" does not appear in *Voyages*.

[38] This is again "4 fathoms" in *Voyages*. It is not likely that Mackenzie set his nets in such deep water.

[39] There seem to be few fisheries on the west side of these islands, for we caught no fish in our crossing. The entire area seems to be one of stone, even the islands and lake bottom, with few feed beds for fish. Fortunately Mackenzie had Indians who knew where to find these few fisheries.

hunting to the By Island opposite, the Weather cloudy, wind changeable, pestered by muskettoes, tho' we are in a manner surrounded by Ice.

SATURDAY 20TH.—Took our Netts up out of the water, no Fish—rained very hard last night and this morning, notwithstanding which Mr. Leroux and People went back to the point that we left the Day before Yesterday, but I could not think to stir as I watch'd the Ice in hopes of its making a Passage. I promised to send for them. Rained at Intervals till about 5 o'clock, we loaded our Canoe and steered for the By Island[40] W. 6 miles, when we came to the point of it at the foot, a Traverse which was full of Ice, we set our Netts and soon caught plenty of Fish. I immediately dispatched 2 young men for Mr. Leroux   Foggy weather. we overtook our Indians on our way here but they had not killed any thing since they left us. I sounded 100 yards from the Island, found 21 fms.[41] There are many Cranberries and Spring onions of which we gathered plenty.

SUNDAY 21ST.—Blew from the Southerd last night   drove the Ice to the Notherd. The 2 Young men returned about 8 this morning. they parted with Mr. Leroux close by, he was obliged to put to shore   blew too hard, I hy'd to take the sun's altitude, and by a glansis of him when it was 12 by my Watch the Lat 61°–34 North   At 2 in the afternoon Mr. Leroux and People [returned?].   at 5 the Ice was almost all drove past to the Northerd, we embarked, making our way thro' much broken Ice steering W. 15 miles on the outside of the Traverse Island and the Ice; the latter seems to be very solid to the N.E.   I sounded 3 times on this distance and found 75·44 and 60 fm Water—we camped upon a small island in the vicinity of many other of the same size (threw out some line and Hook) and within 3 miles of the main land,[42]

40 "Large island," in *Voyages.*

41 Here Mackenzie uses an abbreviation suggesting "fathom." It would seem, therefore, that he knew the difference between feet and fathoms. *Voyages* also uses "fathom" here.

42 Adding the total miles Mackenzie gives for this "island hopping" leads one to conclude that the lake is forty-six miles wide at this point, which is not true. It is about thirty-six miles as the crow flies from Grant Point to the opposite shore. This is

which the Ice prevented our getting to, we espied some Rein Deer upon one of the neighboring Islands. Our Hunters went in pursuit of them and kill'd 5 large and 2 small ones, which was not difficult matter. the poor creatures having no place to run to for Shelter. In consequence of this Capture the Island were named *Isle de Carribo*.[43] I sat up all this night reading to observe the suns setting and Rising   he was under our Horizon 4 Hrs. 22 min; Rose N. 20 E. by Comass.[44] Froze so hard during his absence that the Lake crusted half a quarter of an Inch thick

MONDAY 22D.—Embarked at half past 3 P.M.[45]   went round on the Outside of the Islands and steered N.W. 13 Miles along the Ice edging for the main land, the wind W., then W. 2 Miles. Blew too hard obliged us to land upon an Island at ½ past 9 A.M. We could just distinguish Land to the S.E. stretching a good distance and about 12 Leagues from us,[46] we did not know whether it be the opposite side of the Lake or Islands. I had an observation at Noon which gave me 61° 53″ North.[47] the variation of the compass about 2 pts   Mr. Leroux's People hid 2 Bags Pemican in the Island (for their return which occasioned it to be named *Is la Cach*.[48] The wind moderating a little we again got under way by half past two in the Afternoon   we steered W. b N. 5½ Hours 18 miles chiefly amongst Islands, and at 8 o'clock camp'd upon a small one.[49] have not passed

another one of the few times Mackenzie is long in miles. Perhaps his weaving among the islands explains the extra miles. It is almost impossible to ascertain where Mackenzie camped while in these island groups.

[43] *Voyages* tries to explain why the reindeer were on the island and calls it Isle de Carreboeuf, which is better French but not as close as the Journal to the Indian name, caribou, of a species of reindeer that inhabits that region.

[44] It seems that this word should be "compass," as it is in *Voyages*. Mackenzie must have forgotten the "p."

[45] Mackenzie must have made an error, as the rest of the day's happenings suggest that this should be "3 A.M."

[46] This must have been the Whaleback Rocks. It could hardly have been the Outpost Islands, which would have been in that direction but at too great a distance to see with the naked eye, and the Journal never speaks of using any type of glass such as binoculars or telescope for seeing at a distance.

[47] Mackenzie would be well above 62° north at this point, near 62° 10″.

[48] "*Isle à la Cache*," in *Voyages*.

[49] Again it is impossible to know exactly where he camped, but it must have been very close to what is presently Yellowknife Bay on the southeast side.

any Ice since 8 this morning. Our Indians could not keep up with us. have not seen them since shortly after we embarked, the Muskettoes are so numerous tho' the Weather is so far from being warm that we cannot rest for them

TUESDAY 23D.—Towards Morning our Indians joined us   they paddled all night, they killed 2 Swans & a goose, we continued our Route this Morning at half past three, steering W. b N. 1½ miles. The wind North. Came to the foot of a Traverse across a deep Bay[50] W. 6 miles.[51] there is a considerable large River falls in at the Bottom of it about 12 miles distant. We found the N.W. S[52] of this Bay formed by a No. of small Islands which were quite full of Ice, but the wind drive it off the land a little that we had a clear passage on the inside of it, we steer S.W. 9 miles,[53] under sail then N.W. nearly, thro' Islands we often Carried Sail, the wind having veered a little to the Eastard, this course 16 miles.[54] Here we landed at half past 2 P.M. at 3 lodges of Red knife Indians some of those that had given parole to Mr. Leroux.[55] They informed us that there were as many more lodges[56] of their Friends not far off, one of them went immediately, they told us this was all we would see at present. that the Slave and Beaver Indians as well [as] others of their Tribe will be here by the time that the Swans cast their Feathers. It rained in Torrent upon us this afternoon

WEDNESDAY 24TH.—Traded above 8 packs good Beaver and muslin[57] with those People (in two hours time)   they are not

[50] Today Yellowknife Bay.

[51] "West five miles," in *Voyages.*

[52] "S" expanded to "side" in *Voyages.*

[53] This would suggest that Mackenzie had gone into Yellowknife Bay several miles before making the "traverse."

[54] The very least this distance could be is twenty miles.

[55] *Voyages* leaves out "some of those that had given parole to Mr. Leroux." Perhaps the printer did not understand these words. These Indians had apparently "promised faith or friendship" (the meaning of parole) to Leroux.

[56] *Voyages* states that "there were many more lodges of their friends," thus giving a completely erroneous impression since Mackenzie says that "there were as many more lodges," which is to say there were only three more.

[57] *Voyages* reads, "M. LeRoux purchased of these Indians upwards of eight packs of good beaver and marten skins." The word in the Journal definitely is "muslin," most likely referring to the cloth traded to the Indians for skins; the words "marten skins" do not appear.

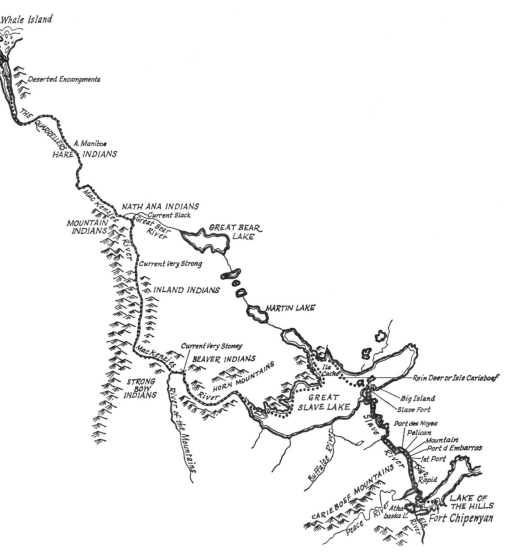

Whale Island

Deserted Encampments.

THE QUARRELLERS

A. Manitoe
HARE INDIANS

Mac Kenzies River

NATH ANA INDIANS
Current Slack
MOUNTAIN
INDIANS
Great Bear River

GREAT BEAR LAKE

Current Very Strong

INLAND INDIANS

MARTIN LAKE

Mackenzies River

Current Very Stoney
BEAVER INDIANS

HORN MOUNTAINS

Ila Cache

Rein Deer or Isle Carieboef

STRONG BOY INDIANS

GREAT SLAVE LAKE

Big Island
Slave Fort

River of the Mountains

River

Port des Noyes
Pelican
Mountain
Port d Embarras
1st Port

Slave River

Buffaloe River

Rapid

CARIEBOEF MOUNTAINS

LAKE OF THE HILLS
Fort Chipewyan

Peace River

River Atha baska L.

Elk River

A MAP OF MACKENZIE'S JOURNEY from Old Fort Chipewyan to the Arctic Ocean. Taken from the 1801 edition of *Voyages*, with original spellings of place names.

above 12 men able to kill Beaver, the English Chief got upwards of 100 Skins from them old Credit outstanding of which he has many in the country, he gave 40 of them to Mr. Leroux as part payment Credits due him since Winter 86–87 at Slave Lake with the rest he bought a few Necessaries and some Rum. and some more I gave him and his young men which made them get Drunk.[58] Had several councils with these since we arrived but could learn nothing material regarding our Expedition, they know nothing even of the River[59] but the Entry. I engaged one of their young men to go and conduct us thither to prevent loss of time in Circumnavigating Bays gave him a pr. of Leggans Brayet Knife & c.,[60] and bought a large new Canoe, that he might embark with the other 2 young men. I had an Observation this Day at noon which gave me 62° 24′ North Latitude.[61] I look upon it that the variation of the Compass is about 26 or 27 Degrees Easterly.

In the afternoon I called the Indians together and informed them that I intended to leave them tomorrow Morning but that Mr. Leroux[62] would remain here till the Indians that they spoke [of] should arrive, and in case they would bring Skins enough to fill his Canoe.[63] that he would send the Frenchmen for more foods in order that he might winter here and build a Fort, which would be continued to them as long as they would deserve it.

[64]They gave me to understand that it would be great encouragement for them to have Frenchmen[65] upon the Land, that they would work hard to kill Beaver, when they would be sure of getting Value for their Skins. that heretofore the Chippiweems always pillaged them whenever they met them (that as they gave them little or

58 *Voyages* does not mention the young men getting "Drunk."

59 This must refer to the Mackenzie River.

60 "I accordingly equipped him with various articles of clothing &c," in *Voyages*.

61 This reading is amazingly close. He was camped, as nearly as I could ascertain, at about 62° 30′ north latitude.

62 "People would remain," in *Voyages*.

63 "Sufficient quantity of skins to make it answer," in *Voyages*.

64 It is very obvious here that the handwriting changes. Also, the paragraphs are now indented in the original, where they were not before.

65 "A settlement of ours" instead of "Frenchmen," in *Voyages*.

nothing in Exchange) which entirely discouraged them from killing Beaver, but when they did it was for the Sake of Food or Rainment. wrote to Messrs. McLeod & McKenzie addressed my Papers to the former to be forwarded by Mr. Leroux le [to?] Athabasca—

THURSDAY 25TH.—parted with Mr. Leroux at 3 this Morning our Canoe very deeply laden having embarked some Ps. that had come in the other Canoe till here. Mr. Leroux got his men & Indians to salute us with several Vollies to which we returned a few Shot, we steered S+. b W. straight across the Bay which is here only 2½ miles wide[66]—by what I cou'd learn from the Natives it's upwards of 40 Leagues[67] Deep and is much wider than what it is here in many Places & full of Islands. In the Traverse I found 6 Fathoms Water, a Sand Bottom. The land on this Side has quite a different appearance from that from where we entered the lake till here. The latter is but one continued View of Mountains & Islands & Solid Rock[68] covered here & there with Moss, Shrubs & Trees, the latter quite stinted in their growth for want of Soil to nourish them; nothwithstanding this barren appearance you can hardly land upon these Rocks but you will meet with gooseberries Cranberries whoilee Berries Brow Berries Juniper Berries, Rasberries, what the Men call *Grains a Perdres* Grain a Saccacamir[69] and what the Indians call *Pythagominan* something like a Rasberry but the last grows upon a small Stalk 1½ ft. high in wet mossy Places all those are in great plenty tho' they do not all grow in one & the same Place.

Then near the lake the land is low & sandy tho' it is well covered with wood of a larger Size, it gets gradually higher & at some distance forms a ridge of high land which appears to run a consider-

[66] The bay is at least four miles wide at the narrowest point in this region.

[67] "Fifteen leagues," in *Voyages*. In actuality, from where Mackenzie was camped, the bay continues northward another thirty-five to sixty miles, depending on whether you include an extension of the bay called Marian Lake.

[68] "High hills and islands of solid rock," in *Voyages*. In actuality the mountains and hills and islands are all solid rock with only occasional shallow soil covering.

[69] *Voyages* lists "partridge berries" as an addition but leaves out "whoilee Berries," "Brow Berries," and "what the men call *Grains a Perdres* Grain a Saccacomir."

able distance along the Coast and has not much wood on Top appears Rocky & Sandy. We steer S.S.E. 9 Miles we are stopped by drifting, with some difficulty we got to an Island where we landed at 7 oClk A.M.   I went to the furthermost End of it to see if we might have any hopes of getting away from here this Day It's about 5 Miles round, I was much surprised to find that the greatest part of the Wood of the Island had been cut down about 12 or 15 Years since & that no part of it remained on the Ground, but the Stumps which were quite rotten, when I returned I enquired of the Indian Chief[70] what was the meaning of this he informed me that several winters ago that this was the land of the Slave Indians & many of them lived upon the Island round this Bay there being an excellent Fishery all the Year thro' that it was the Crees[71] that drove them away from here by frequently coming to War upon them. If Mr. Leroux[72] winters in this Country he is to build near this Place on acct. of the Fishery & wood.[73] At 11 oclock A.M. the wind having drove the greatest part of the Ice past the Island, we made our way thro' some Broken Ice tho' at the risk of damaging our Canoe. Steering S.E. from Point to point across 5 Bays 21 Miles I sounded several Times & found from 6 to 16 fm water.[74] I observ'd that the Inland Country got gradually lower [word scratched out] but better covered with Wood than where it was higher   upon every part of the Land that we came near to were old lodges. The Hunters kill'd 2 Swan and a Beaver. We landed at 8 oclk unloaded & gummed our Canoe as usual &c.[75]

FRIDAY 26TH.—we landed & continued our Rout (5 oclk) Steering S.E. for 10 miles across 2 deep Bays. Then S.S.E.   Islands in Sight to the Eastward   travers'd another Bay 3 Miles, then S. 1

[70] "English Chief," in *Voyages*.

[71] "Knistenaux"—which are a branch of the Crees—in *Voyages*.

[72] "An establishment" instead of "Mr. Leroux," in *Voyages*.

[73] This island is presently known as Old Fort. It has considerable forest on it and also a winter commercial fishing camp.

[74] "Six to ten fathom," in *Voyages*.

[75] It is very difficult to know exactly where Mackenzie camped on this particular evening since there are bays within bays along this shore line. Certainly he was still in the North Arm of Great Slave lake.

mile to a point which we named the delour,[76] S.S.W. 4½ Miles a heavy Swol of the Lake. had an observation here 61°.40 North Lat: S.W. 4 miles, W.S.W. among Islands. Our Indians kill'd 2 Rein Deer upon one of those Islands, we lost 3 Hours aft wind going for them. This Course about 9 miles   abt. 7 P.M. obliged to Land for the Night[77] the wind too strong from the S.E.   we thought we could observe land in this Direction when the Wind was coming on. From some Distance on the other Side the Detoar the land is low & the land is very flat & dangerous there being no safe place of landing in case of bad weather except in the Islands we just past. There seem to be plenty of Moos & Rein Deer in this Country, we saw the tracks every where we landed. likewise Number of White Partridges are now almost all grey of the Colour of the Moorefull[78] Saw some floating Ice to Day on the lake. The Indians killed 2 Swan.

N.B. My Steersman had a misunderstanding with his Lady last night & arranged her to remain at the Campmt. but his Cousin (her Furreaux) got her on board & the Husband said nothing to the contrary[79]

SATURDAY 27TH.—By 3 this morning we were under way after a very restless Night being tormented with Musquittoes. A fine Calm our Course—W.S.W. 9 miles   here we came to the foot of a Traverse the opposite Point in St. bearing S.W. distance 12 Miles.[80] This Bay is at least 8 miles deep[81] this Course 2 Miles more, it came on very foggy and as there were so many Bays we landed till it

[76] *Voyages* calls this point "Detour" and probably this is what the Journal should say since the word "Detoar" is used later. The point is most likely Edgar Point, just about two miles south and a little west of Gypsum Point. Mackenzie would be leaving the North Arm and entering the main lake here.

[77] This campsite must have been somewhere on the shore behind or near present-day Long Island. Mackenzie's estimation of mileage here is much better but still slightly short.

[78] "Moor-fowl," in *Voyages*.

[79] This little human-interest story is left out of *Voyages*.

[80] This bay must be Lonely Bay. From Lonely Point to Northwest Point, across the mouth of the bay, is eight or at the most nine miles.

[81] In this passage, the words "deep," "bottom," etc. obviously refer to distance rather than vertical depth.

would clear up, which it did in 2 Hours time which we took the advantage of [by?] steering S. 13 Miles past several small Bays, here we came to the point of a very deep one, the land drowned towards the Bottom the opposite Side bearing S. from us distance 10 miles our guides quite at a loss they do not know what course to take he says its 8 winters since he has been here, that this Bay is much like the Entrance of the River in consequence we steered down the Bay[82] about W.S.W. Course till we got in amongst Fields of Broken Ice still we could not see the Bottom of the Bay nor could we proceed. The Fog coming on made it very difficult for us to get to an Island S.W. of us, it was near dark when we landed upon it & camped.

SUNDAY 28TH.—At a Quarter past 3 this Morning we were on the Water and as we could perceive no current Setting into this Bay, we made the best of our way to the Point that bore South of us yesterday Afternoon S. 3 Miles more, then S. b W. 7 miles, W. 15 Miles.[83] had an observation 61 Degrees N. Lat: W.N.W. 2 Miles here we came to the foot of a Traverse the opposite land bearing S.W. Distance 14 Miles[84] this being a deep Bay we steered into it about a westerly Course having no Land in St. a head in hopes to find a Passage which the Indian informed us was to be met with before we came to the Grand River having a strong aft wind we lost sight of the Indians nor could we put ashore to wait for them without running the Risk of wrecking our Canoe till we came to the bottom of the Bay and ran our Canoe in amongst Bushes,[85] but we found there was no Passage here. in two or three Hours time they join'd us but would not come near our Fire this being not a good Campment, they emptied their Canoe of the Water they had taken in & continued their Route & we followed.[86] did not Camp till Sunset. the English Chief was in a great Passion with the Red

---

[82] This must be Sulphur Bay.

[83] Actually Mackenzie was going northwest from Slave Point. The distance is about fifteen miles. The north latitude at that point would have been about 61° 15'.

[84] Here the low banks around the North Channel fooled Mackenzie. The distance, which is greatly distorted in Deep Bay, is only about ten miles.

[85] "Forced among the rushes," in *Voyages*.

[86] "We followed" is left out of *Voyages*.

Knif wanted to shoot him for having undertaken to guide us in a Road he did not know, indeed none of us are well pleased with him, but we don't think with the English Chief that he merits such severe punishm't. besides he gave us some hopes that we are close by the River, that he recollects to have passed from the River thro' the wood to the Place that we landed at.[87]

MONDAY 29TH.—Embarked at 4 oclk this Morning[88] steering along the S.W. Side of the Bay   at ½ past 5 we came to the extremity of the point which we doubled & found it to be the Passage we were in search of, occasioned by a very long Island which separated this from the Main Channel of the River, It is about ½ a Mile[89] across not above 6 foot deep we could observe a vast many Fish in the water & the Place was almost covered with wild Fowl, Swan, Geese & several kinds of Ducks & particularly Black Ducks were very numerous, but we cou'd not get within gunshot of any of them,[90] the Currt. set us at S.W. b W. not very strong   followed the Course till we passed the Pt. of the long Island (where the River is upward of 10 miles across) 14 Miles   there is from 1 to 2 ft[91] water & I suppose when The water is low in the lake the greater part of this Channel must be dry. Now the River turns W. (gradually getting narrower) 24 Miles,[92] here it is not above a Mile[93] wide but the Current is much stronger, sounded, found 3½ fms the land on the N. Shore from the Lake here is low & well wooded, that on the South appears higher and has plenty of wood on it likewise. The current is very strong, the Banks are equally high on

[87] *Voyages* adds, "In the blowing weather to-day, we were obliged to make use of our large kettle, to keep our canoe from filling, although we did not carry above three feet sail. The Indians very narrowly escaped."

[88] "Evening," in *Voyages*.

[89] It is, in fact, well over a mile across, but it is quite shallow.

[90] The area is still heavily populated with wild fowl which are very easily frightened.

[91] "From five to two fathom," in *Voyages*, which is obviously incorrect, for the water is very shallow.

[92] Mackenzie is long on mileage here, perhaps because of the very low shore line, which is extremely misleading. Mackenzie estimates the distance from the entrance of the North Channel to Dory Point as thirty-eight miles when in reality it is under thirty miles.

[93] "Half a mile wide," in *Voyages*. The Journal is nearer the actual distance.

both Sides, yellow clay mix'd with Stones & covered with much
Bur't wood upon the Ground & young Aspin Trees that have grown
since the Fire passed.[94] have a stiff breeze from the Eastward w'ch
drove us on at a great Rate under sail, our Course about the same
tho' winding among Islands, we keep the North Channel where the
Current is much stronger.   that in the South Channel does not
appear to be so much, so of course will be the easiest Road to come
up, 10 miles,[95] here the River widens, the wind dies away & we
have recourse to our Paddles, we keep the North Side of the River
our Course N.W.   the River is very wide here in form of a small
Lake, we cou'd see no opening in any Direction so that we are at
a loss what course to take. Our Red Knif Indian has never been
further than this; A River falls in from the N. and as he says takes
its rise in the Horn Mountain the land of the Beaver Indians. that
he and his Relation met with some of them upon this River that
there are very extensive Plains on both Sides the ["island" crossed
out] Grand River abounding with Buffaloes & Moor Deer.[96] By
keeping this Course we came into Shallow water which made us
steer to the left, till we came into deeper water which we followed
till the channel of the River opened to us to the Southd.   we made
for the Shore & we Camp'd after Sun Set.[97] Our Course ought to
have been W. 15 Miles since we took the Paddle. The Horn Mountain in Sight—being N.W. from us & running N.N.E. & S.S.W.
I sounded frequently to Day   found from 3 to 6 fm. Water. Our

[94] *Voyages* adds, "It is a very curious and extraordinary circumstance, that land
covered with spruce, pine, and white birch, when laid waste by fire, should sub-
sequently produce nothing but poplars, where none of that species of tree were pre-
viously to be found." (Poplar is used instead of "aspin.") This interpolation reveals
Combe's lack of understanding of the vegetation in this northern area. Pine, spruce,
and birch will grow again after being burned down, but their growth is much slower
than poplar, and frequently poplar will stunt or choke out the other wood for some
time.

[95] The speed of the current completely fooled Mackenzie. Here the river flows
about eight to ten miles an hour. The distance he covered was about twenty-five miles.

[96] *Voyages* states that he and his relations "frequently meet on that river," and
also adds that "there are very extensive plains on both sides of it, which abound in
buffaloes and moose deer." This would give the impression of frequent meetings,
while the Journal suggests only one meeting.

[97] Mackenzie covered over eighty miles this first day on the river.

Hunters kill'd 2 Geese & a Swan—Vast Nrs. of Fowl breeding in those Islands—

TUESDAY 30TH.—at 4 this Morning we got under Way   a fine Calm. Our Course S.W. b S. 36 Miles, upon the South Side of the River is a ridge of low Mountains[98] running East & West by Compass. The Indians pick'd up a white Brant which appeared to have been Shot with a Bow & Arrow & quite Fresh. S.W. b W. 6[99] Miles   A Bay upon our left full of small Islands & by appearance the Entrance of a River from the South & the ridge of Mountains terminates here. This Course for 15 Miles   at 6 P.M. appearance of bad weather. we landed for the Night[100] & before we could pitch our Tents it came on a violent Tempest, of Thunder, Lightening, wind & Rain, which ceased in a little Time after giving us a compleat soaking, which the men and Indians are not so much displeased with it being the means of their camping a couple of Hours earlier than they would otherwise have done[101] & the latter are very much fatigued having ran much after wild Fowl, which have cast their Feathers. They caught 6 Swan and 5 Geese. I sounded several times today   found from 4 to 6 fm. Water

JULY 1789

WEDNESDAY JULY 1ST.—loaded and push'd off at a quarter before 4 A.M.[1] Soon the River narrows to about ½ mile over, our Course W. amongst Islands,[2] a strong Current the land high on both sides but the Banks are not perpendicular, this Course 21 Miles, sounded 9 fms   then W.N.[3] 9 Miles, passed a River upon the S.E. side Sounded again 12 fms   N.W. b W. 3 Miles; here I lost my lead and part of my line it getting fast at the Bottom   the Current

[98] High hills might be a better term.

[99] "South-West by South six miles," in *Voyages*, which is not as nearly accurate as the Journal.

[100] His mileage and general information for this day are amazingly accurate. He failed only to realize that he was slowly turning northward.

[101] *Voyages* leaves out from "which the men" to "otherwise have done."

[1] "At half past four in the morning," in *Voyages*.

[2] By this time Mackenzie is going almost directly northwest.

[3] "West-North-West," in *Voyages*. Actually they turned a little east of north.

is too strong to steer'd (in order to get it clear) with 8 Paddles,[4] as a Man could not break it   N. b W. 5 Miles, a high Mountain bearing South from us N.W. b N. 4 Miles, pass a small River on the N. side then steer'd round a point to W.S.W.   at one oClock there came on Thunder, lightening, wind, and Rain, which ceased in about ½ an Hour and left us wet to the Skin as we did not land. Great Quantities of Ice along the Banks of the River. Landed upon a small Island where there were the Poles of 4 lodges, which we concluded to have been Crees, upon their War Excursions by appearance 6 or 7 years since. This Course for 15 Miles[5] then W. where the River of the Mountain[6] falls in from the Southerd   It appears to be a large River upwards of ½ Mile[7] over, at the Entry. About 6 miles further a small River[8] from the same Direction, this course 24 Miles   we landed opposite to an Island   the Mountains to the Southerd in St.   as our Canoe is very deep laden and that we are in daily Expectations of coming to the Rapids, which we have been made to dread, we hid 2 Bags of pemican in the opposite Island which I expect may be of Service to us in time to come, tho' our Indians are of a difft. opinion, they having no Expectations of coming back here, this Season, of course it will be lost   Close by are two Indian Campments of last Years   by their way of Cutting the wood they must have had no Iron works. The Currt. was very strong all Day   the Indians killed 2 Swans[9]

TUESDAY [THURSDAY?] 2D.—A very thick Fog this morning, embarked at half past 5 P.M.[10] cleared up at 7   the water has changed from being limpid to muddy, which we suppose must be

[4] *Voyages* adds "and the strength of the line, which was equal to four paddles." It leaves out "as a Man could not break it."

[5] He must be referring here to the relatively straight stretch of river which flows in a westerly but slightly northerly direction from Strong Point to Fort Simpson.

[6] Today the Liard River.

[7] It is well over a mile wide.

[8] The Martin River. He was at this point going approximately northwest, but he thought he was going west.

[9] This day Mackenzie's figures suggest that he traveled between eighty-five and ninety miles. In reality he traveled at least one hundred miles.

[10] The writer must mean "A.M." since "9 oClock A.M." is used later.

owing to some large River falling in from the Southerd[11] which the Fog prevented our seeing, at 9 oClock A.M. perceive very high Mountains ahead and upon our nearer approach at a No. of very high Hills. the Tops of them hid in the Clouds ran as far as our view could carry to the Southerd. At Noon lightening, Thunder and Rain, at 1 oclock came a Breast of the Mountains,[12] they appear Barren and Rocky upon Top, but well covered with Wood towards the Bottom, there appears a No. of white Stones upon them which glistens when the Rays of the sun shines upon them. The Indians say they are *Maneloe Aseniah*,[13] but I think they must be Talk,[14] tho' they are rather whiter that I have ever seen[15] our Course has been W.S.W.[16] 30 miles   we went on very cautiously here expecting every moment that we would come to some great rapid or Fall, we were so full of this that every person in his turn thought he heard a noise & the falling of water,[17] which only subsisted in our Imaginations, our course changes to W. b N.[18] along the Mountains 12 miles N. b W. 21[19] mile   at 8 oClock P.M. put on shore for the Night[20] upon the North side   we saw many of the Natives Campments today some of them of this Spring and others older. The Hunters killed a swan and a Beaver the first

[11] There is no large river falling into the Mackenzie here, but many small ones. The river also widens in this area several times, with low muddy banks suggesting a muddy bottom rather than sand.

[12] Today the Camsell Range.

[13] *"Manetoe aseniah*, or spirit stones," in *Voyages*.

[14] He more likely means "talc."

[15] *Voyages* adds "on our return, however, these appearances were dissolved, as they were nothing more than patches of snow." These lines do not appear in the Journal even in the entries made on the return trip. Besides, the mountains do have these white, talc-like stones in them, and one does get quite near enough to tell that it is not snow.

[16] All this time he has been going in a northwesterly direction.

[17] Mackenzie's group must have allowed their imaginations to run wild, for although the current is moderately swift the river runs smoothly with no noise. He might have been trying to get a little suspense into his narrative.

[18] His course changed to slightly east of due north.

[19] This is still almost due north.

[20] It is very difficult to know his exact place of encampment for this evening. He suggests he has traveled some sixty-three miles, but my guess is that he traveled nearer eighty miles and camped not far from the present-day Willow Lake River.

that we have seen since we have been in the River, The Indians complain much of our hard Marching, that they are not accustomed to such hard fatigue.

FRIDAY 3D.—Rained all last night and till 7 this morn'g when we embarked and steered N.N.W. for 12 miles,[21] high Mountains on both sides of the River, a strong head wind, rained hard, obliged us to land at 10 oClock A.M.   by my reckoning since my last observation, we have ran 217 Miles West and 44 Miles[22] N.   at a quarter past 2 P.M. the Rain subsided, and we got again under way, our Course as before for 5 miles, here a River falls in from the N.   soon after the Currt. became strong and rapid amongst Rocky Islands, the first that we saw in this River, and which we thought a sure indication of soon meeting with Falls and Rapids   Our present Course N.W. b N. for 10 Miles then N.W. 3 miles W.N.W. 12 miles, N.W. 3 miles[23] and Camped at 8 oClk at the foot of a high Hill[24] on the North Shore part of it perpendicular with the River   I ascended it accompanied by 2 men and also Indians   it took us an hour and a quarter[25] hard walking, I was very much surprised to find a Campment on top of it, the Indians told me that it is the Custom of all the People who have no arms to make choice of Places of this Kind for their residence, as they could easily make them inaccessible to their Enemies particularly those who the Crees make war on, they being in continual dread of them. Our view was not so extensive as we had expected it being terminated all round with such Hills as the one we were upon   between the Hills are Nos. of small Lakes upon which we could perceive many Swans, the Country appeared very thinly wooded, a few Trees of the Pine and Birch, and very small in Size, we were obliged to shorten our Stay here on account

[21] He is still going almost due north.

[22] By this time he had traveled well over one hundred miles north and nearly two hundred miles west.

[23] Actually the river does make a great bend westward here to present-day Wrigley.

[24] This hill is directly across the river from Wrigley. Mackenzie's estimated mileage for this day was approximately right.

[25] "About an hour and a half," in *Voyages*.

of the Swarms of Muskettoes that attacked us and were the only Inhabitants of the Place. We saw many of the Natives Encampments this Day, none of them of this years. Since 4 oClk P.M. the Current has been excessive strong so much so that it makes such a hissing and Ebbition as a little moderately Boiling.[26] The weather has been cold all Day, which is more sensible to us as it was very Sultry before, since we have been in the River.

SATURDAY 4TH.—at 5 A.M. put off. Wind and Weather as Yesterday. Steer N.W. b N.[27] 22 Miles N.W. 6 miles N.W. b N. 4 miles W.N.W. 5 miles pass a small River from the North, turn round a point S.W. 1 mile N.W. 4 Miles[28] A River from the South N.N.W. a Mountain a head 15 Miles. 2 Rivers opposite one another.[29] W. 4 Miles N.W. 13 Miles.[30] At 8 oClk P.M. Camped upon an Island, the current as strong all day as it was yesterday afternoon. a quantity of Ice along the Banks of River, the Indians killed a goose, and the Men a Beaver which sunk before we could get him.[31]

SUNDAY 5TH.—Last night the sun set at 55 minutes[32] past 9 by my watch, and rose before 2 this morning, we embarked soon after steering N.N.W. thro' Islands for 5 miles W. 4 miles,[33] the River widens, and the Current slackens a little N.W. 5 Miles, perceive

[26] *Voyages* states: "Since four in the afternoon the current has been so strong that it was, at length, in an actual ebullition, and produced an hissing noise like a kettle of water in a moderate state of boiling." The water does make a hissing noise at the side of your canoe in places, but it is not loud, and it was continuous as we went through this area. Had the water been higher it is possible it would have been more pronounced.

[27] "North-West by West twenty-two miles," in *Voyages*. The Journal direction is more nearly correct.

[28] "N.W. 4 miles" is omitted in *Voyages*.

[29] These must be the Saline River and the Redstone River.

[30] Mackenzie had traveled this day much further north than west and much further north than he realized. He reckoned the day's travel to be about seventy-five miles, whereas in reality he had traveled over one hundred miles. He must have camped somewhere near Dry Island.

[31] *Voyages* adds "beaver, otters, bears, &c, if shot dead at once, remain like a bladder, but if there remains enough of life for them to struggle, they soon fill with water and go to the bottom."

[32] "Fifty-three minutes past nine" and "seven minutes before two this morning," in *Voyages*.

[33] He actually went almost directly north and then west.

a ridge of high snowy Mountains ahead W.S.W. 10 miles[34] and at ¾ past 7 Oclock we perceived several Smokes, which we made for with all speed, soon saw the Natives run about in great Confusion, some making the woods and others to their Canoes. Our Hunters landed before us and spoke to the few that had not been quick enough to run away, in the Chipewean Language which at first they could not understand thro' the confusion they were in, but they saw it was impossible for them to make their Escape as we were all landed   they made signs to us for to keep at a Distance, which we did and unloaded our Canoe and pitched our Tents before any of us went near them, during which time the English Chief and his young men were very busy in reconciling them to our arrival, for when the Flurry was over, and they saw we intended them no hurt, it was found that some of the Men understood our Indians very well, who persuaded them to come down to where we were which they consented to with great Reluctance and not without evident Signs of Fear, but the Reception they met with partly removed their Terror. and they recalled the rest of their People from their hiding Places. there are 5 families of them in all, 26 or 30 Persons, and of two diftr. Tribes, Slave and Dog Rib Indian, we made them smoke, tho' it was evident they did not know the use of Tobacco, we likewise gave them some grog to drink, but I believe they accepted of those Civilities more through Fear than Inclination by the Distribution of Knives, beads, awls, Rings, garlering,[35] Fire Steels, Flints and a couple of Axes, they became more familiar than we expected, for we could not keep them out of our Tents, tho' I did not observe that they tryed to steal anything from us— The Information they gave us respecting the River, seems to me so very *fabulous* that I will be particular in inserting. Suffice it to say that they would wish to make us believe that we would be several Winters getting to the Sea, and that we all should be old men by the time we would return. that we would have to encounter many

[34] In reality Mackenzie was traveling in a direction slightly north of west and landed very near to the present Fort Norman.

[35] "Gartering," in *Voyages*.

Portrait of Sir Alexander Mackenzie in the Mackenzie House in Montreal.
Probably a modern copy of an 1800 portrait by Sir Thomas Lawrence, in
the National Gallery of Canada, Ottawa. The signature under the portrait
is from a document in the McCord Museum, McGill University.

Ice packs on the Athabasca River.

The harbor of New Fort Chipewyan. Old Fort Point, not visible, lies on the horizon about twenty miles away.

The entrance to the Rochers River, reached by Mackenzie on
June 3, 1789.

One of the many rapids around which Mackenzie had to portage on June 5.

The "Portage d Embarass occasioned by driftwood" which Mackenzie
encountered on June 5, still present in 1965.

Mackenzie's mountain portage "350 paces long" of June 5.

The entrance to Great Slave Lake from the Jean River, where Mackenzie
arrived on June 9.

Monsters (which can only exist in their own while Imaginations)
Besides that there are 2 impracticable Falls or Rapids in the
River, the first 30 Days March from us &c. &c.   Tho' I put no
faith in those Stories, they had a different Effect upon the English
Chief, and his young men (who were already very tired of their
voyage) It was their Opinion and wish that we should absolutely
return, adding to the above Reasons many others—that they were
informed that there were very few animals below this, and the
farther we went the fewer there would be, of course that we should
Starve, even if no other Accident befell us. I with much ado dis-
suaded them out of their Reasonings and made them to ask one[36]
of the Natives to accompany us, which they soon did, one of the
others as soon consented to in Consideration of getting a Small
Kettles, Axe, Trencher, Knife &c. Altho' it was now 3 oClk in the
afternoon I wanted to make the most of our time   I order'd My[37]
Men to reload in our Canoe & as soon as we were ready to embark
called upon our new Recruit to do the same, which he would rather
have declined, however as none of his Friends would take his place,
& after the loss of an hours time we in a manner compelled him to
embark, previous to his departure I observ'd a piece of Ceremony
of which I could not learn the meaning, he cut a lock of his Hair
separated it into 3 Parts one of which he fastened to the hair of the
crown of his Wifes head, blowing on it three times as hard as he
could & repeating some words, the other two he fastened with the
same Ceremony on the heads of his two children. During our short
stay with those People they amused us with Dancing to their own
Vocal music, in neither of which there is no great variety, at least
as far as we cou'd perceive—They form a Ring Men & women
promiscuously, the former have a Bone Dagger or piece of Stick
between the fingers of the Right Hand which they keep extended
above the head & in continual motion, the left they seldom raise
so high but keep working backward & forward in a horizontal direction keeping time to their Music. They jump & put themselves into

[36] In the Journal, "one" is inserted with a caret before "of."
[37] In the Journal, "My" is written clearly over "our."

different Antic Shapes, keeping their Heels close together, at every pause they make the Men give a howl in Imitation of the Wolf, or some other Animal & those that hold out the longest at this strong exercise seem to pass for the best Performers;[38] the Women hang their Arms as if without the Power of Motion—They are all an ugly meagre ill made People particularly about the Legs which are very clumsy & full of Scabs by their frequent roasting them to the Fire. Many of them appear'd very sickly owing as I imagine to their Dirty way of living. They are of the Middle Stature & as Far as could be discerned thro' Dust & grease that cover their whole Body fairer than the generality of Indians, who inhabit warmer climes Some of them wear their hair long, others have it long behind & from the Crown down to the two Ears cut quite short, but none of them take any pains to keep it in order, a few of the old men had their beards long & the rest had it pulled out by the Roots that not a hair was to be seen. The Men have two double Lines Black or Blue tatoed upon each Cheek from Ear to Nose, the Gristle of the latter is perforated large enough to admit a goose quille, which or a piece of Stick some of them had passed in the orifice. They make their Clothing of the Skin of the Rein or Moor Deer[39] well dressed but the Skin of the first is more Common & they dress many of them in the Hair for winter wear, of either they make Shirts which come down half their Thighs some of which they embroider very neatly with Porcupines Quills & the Hair of the Moor Deer[40] painted Red, Black, Yellow & White (say cold.) their Robes are large enough to cover a Man & serve for that purpose asleep or awake, they are fringed round at Bottom their edging[41] comes up half the Thigh & are of a Piece with the shoes, they are embroidered round the ancle and upon every Seam; the Women dress the same

---

[38] *Voyages* describes this part of the dance thus: ". . . while they leap about and throw themselves into various antic postures, to the measure of their music, always bringing their heels close to each other at every pause. The men occassionaly howl in imitation of some animal, and he who continues this violent exercise for the longest period, appears to be considered as the best performer."
[39] "Moose-deer," in *Voyages.*
[40] "Moose," in *Voyages.*
[41] "Legging" instead of "edging," in *Voyages.*

as the men. The Men have no covering on their Private Parts except a small Tassel of Parings of Leather, which hang loose by a small Cord, before them in order as I think to keep off the Flies which otherwise wo'd be very troublesome, both young and old men have the glans of the Penis uncovered indeed their want of Modesty & their having no Sense of their Nakedness but from the Cold would make a Person think that they were descended from Adam, and probably had he been created at the Arctic Circles he would not have had occasion for Eve, the Serpent, nor the Tree of Knowledge to have given him a Sense of his Nakedness[42]

Their ornaments consists of Bracelets, gorgets, Arm & wrist Bands made of wood, Horn, or Bone, Belts garters & a kind of a Cap which they wear on the Head made of a Piece of Leather 1½ Ins wide embroider'd with Porcupines Quills & stuck round with the Claws of Bears or wild Fowls inverted to each of which hangs a few parings of fine white Ferrit Skins[43] in fashion of a Tassel, the Cinchures of garters[44] are of Porcupine Quills wove with Sinews & are the neatest thing of the kind that ever I saw, some others they make of Common Quills which are not so handsome; to both kinds they fasten a long fringe which are made by working the Hair of the original of different Colours round strings of Leather.[45] Their Lodges are as simple as as can be imagined, a few Poles laid across one another supported by a Fork & forming a Demi Circle[46] at bottom Covered with a few Branches or a Piece or Two of Bark under which they sleep[47]—they make two of those Structures facing one another & make the fire between. their Furniture is of a Piece with their lodgings, two or three Dishes of Wood, Bark, or horn, the Vessel which serve them to cook their Victuals are something of the Shape of a Gourd wide & bulged below & narrower at Top made

---

[42] *Voyages* leaves out the previous lines from "indeed" to "Nakedness."

[43] *Voyages* adds "an animal that resembles the ermine."

[44] "Cinctures and garters," in *Voyages*.

[45] *Voyages* adds "Their mittens are also suspended from the neck in a position convenient for the reception of the hands."

[46] "Semicircle," in *Voyages*.

[47] The reference to sleep is left out of *Voyages*.

of Wallup[48] Basket work, but so close that it holds Water with any other thing they chuse to put in it, They make it boil by putting a sufficiency of Red hot Stones into it. those Vessels contain from 2 to 6 gals.   They have a Number of Small Leather Bags to hold their embroidered work, Lines, Nets, Willow Bark of which they always have a Quantity by them, they work this Bark into Thread upon their Thigh. their Nets are from 3 to 40 fm. long 13 to 36 Meshes deep, the short deep ones they set in the Eddy Current in the River & the long ones in the Lakes. they likewise make Lines of the Sinews of Rein Deer, their Hooks of Wood, Horn, or Bone, their Arms & hunting weapons are Bows & Arrows, Spears, Daggs, & pogmagans,[49] the Bows are about 5 or 6 ft. long the Strings of Sinew or Green Skin, the Arrows 2½ ft. long including the Point which is of bone, Horn, Stone Iron or Copper, they are feathered at the End with three Feathers. the handle of the Spears are about 6 foot long pointed with a barbed Bone 10 Inches long, with this they Spear the Rein Deer in the water; the Daggs are about 12 inches long flat & sharp pointed made of Bone or Horn. the Pogmagan is made of the Horn of Rein Deer the Branches all cut off but one towards the extremity   this is left 4 Inches long. This Machine is upwards of 2 ft. long & serve to them to dispatch their Enemies in Battle & such animals as they catch with Snares. those Snares are 3 fms long made of the green Skin of the Rein or Moor Deer cut so that it requires from 10 to 30 Strand to make this Cord which is not thicker than a Cod Line & strong enough to resist the Strength of any Animal in the Country. they make Snares of Sinews with which they catch Hares & white Partridges which are exceeding numerous in this Country, their Axes are made of a Piece of brown or grey Stone 6 or 8 Ins. long Sqr.[50] left flat on the inside rounded on the Out Side & tapering to a pt. or Edge an Inch wide, they fasten it by the Middle flat Side inward to a handle 2 ft. long with a Cord of Green Skin & altho' a tedious Work cut & split their Wood with this

[48] *Voyages* uses here "of watape" and explains in a footnote that it is from the "roots of the spruce-fir."

[49] The last two weapons are "daggers, and pogamagans, or clubs" in *Voyages*.

[50] *Voyages* has also "two inches thick."

Tool.[51] they make Fire by striking together a Piece of White or Yellow Pirclis[52] & a Flint Stone over a Piece of dry Punk.[53] Young & old are provided with the Materials and in an Instant strike fire, they have small bits of Iron which they get from the next Tribe to them, those from the Red Knives & Chippiweans in barter for Martin Skins & a few Beaver—they make knives of those small bits of Iron by fixing them in the End of a small Stick   with those & Beaver Teeth they finish all their Work   they have them in a Sheath hanging on their Neck.[54] Always ready to run their hand into them—Their Canoes are small, pointed at both Ends, flat bottomed cover'd before all made of the Bark of the Birch Tree & Fir wood, quite slight & so light that they carry them over Land wherever they go—seldom more than One Person embarks in them, nor can they carry above two, the Paddles are 6 ft long half of which is the Blade about 8 Ins wide; we learn from those People that we had passed Numbers of Indians who inhabit the Mountains on the East Side of the River. We parted from them at 4 o Clk P.M. they promised to remain upon the Banks of the River till the fall in case we should come back. Our Course S.S.W.[55] we soon passed the River of the great Bear Lake which appears to be a fine deep River abt. 100 yds.[56] wide, the water is quite clear of the colour of Salt Water (Sea)   we did not go above 6 miles when we were obliged to land for the Night by a very heavy gust of wind with Rain. Our Campment is under a high Hill or Rock, our new Conductor told us that it blew every day in the Year on the Top of this Hill,[57] he was very uneasy with us, pretending sickness that

[51] *Voyages* adds "and we believe, the only one of its kind among them."

[52] "Pyrites," in *Voyages*.

[53] *Voyages* uses "touchwood," a term I'm sure the Indians or the *voyageurs* never used.

[54] In *Voyages*, "Always ready to run their hand in them" is left out, and in its place is inserted "which also contains their awls both of iron and horn."

[55] Actually he would have been going a little north of west.

[56] The River is about a quarter of a mile wide.

[57] The island in the river in front of Mackenzie's camp is known today as Windy Island. He is again short on mileage, having made at least forty miles that day rather than thirty.

we might let him return to his relations to prevent which We be obliged to watch him all Night.

MONDAY 6TH.—very Cloudy raw weather this morning at 3 oclock A.M. we embarked steering W.S.W. 4 Miles W. 4 Miles,[58] W. b S. 16 Miles, W. 27 Miles, S.W. 9 Miles, then W. 6 Miles[59] & Camp'd at half past 7 P.M. we passed thro' many Islands to day the Ridge of Snowy Mountains always in Sight. Our Stranger informed us that there are a great Number of Bears & white Buffaloes (small) in the Mountains & that they are inhabited, we camp'd under a high Rocky Hill which I attempted to ascent accompanied by one of the Young Hunters but we were obliged to relinquish our design half way up it being nearly suffocated by Swarms of Musquittoes. I cou'd see that the Mountain terminated here at least as far as we cou'd see & a River falling in from the Westwd.[60] Observed a strong Rapling Current or rapid close by under the Hill which then was a Precipice.

TUESDAY 7TH.—Embarked at 4 oclock A.M. crossed to the opposite Side on account of the Rapid I mentioned above but we might have saved ourselves the trouble as there was no danger in going Streight down it, this proved to be one of the dangerous Rapids we had to pass & convinced me in my Opinion respecting the falsity of the Natives Information. Our Course N.N.W. for three Miles W.N.W. 4 Miles N.W. 10 Miles N. 2 Miles[61] a small River from the East Side where we landed 4 Fires The People ran off excepting an Old Man & Woman notwithsd. our Conductor called to them but they cou'd neither see nor hear him, the old Man came down to meet us telling us that he was pitifully worn

58 *Voyages* adds "West-North-West five miles, west eight miles."

59 Except for the first few miles and the last few miles, which were almost due west, Mackenzie traveled this day in general northwest. The Journal suggests he traveled 66 miles while he really traveled some 110 miles. He camped at the head of the Sans Sault Rapids.

60 Whether this is the Carcajou River or Mountain River is difficut to ascertain since they enter the Mackenzie River within a mile or two of each other.

61 Here Mackenzie was only a very few miles from what today is known as the Ramparts. To get there from the Sans Sault Rapids he would have gone north, then northwest, again north, and finally swung into the northeast. He seems to get farther off as he moves north, mainly, it seems, because he felt he was going westward all the time.

out with old age & for the time he had to live it was not worth while for him to run away, he began to pull out his Grey Hairs by hand-fuls distributing it amongst us begging that we should have Mercy on him & his relations   at last our Indian[62] made him listen to him and partly removed his fear   he called back his relations in all 18 People, I made them Presents of Knives, Beads, Awls &c. which pleased them exceedingly, they differed in no respect from those that we had seen and they offered us Fish to eat which was very well boiled and accepted of, with a few they had just caught, we were obliged to force our guide to embark, he wanted abso-lutely to return, we learned from those People that we were close by the other great rapid, and that there were several lodges of their relations there. 4 Canoes followed us a man in each to shew us where to take the Road to go down the rapid. They like the other people told us many discouraging Stories, our Course from here N.N.E. 2 Miles, the River appeared quite shut up with high per-pendicular white Rocks, this did not at all please us, we went ashore to try to visit the rapid, but there was no possibility of seeing any thing, the Indians made a great Noise about it, but at last we thot. when they ventured to go down it with their small Canoes, we might venture it with ours, so we followed them at a small distance, we came between the steep Rock I mention as above but did not find the Current stronger than elsewhere, we were still in Expectation of coming to the rapid till they told us there was no other but what we saw. the River is not above 300 yds overhere,[63] I sounded and found 50 fms water, at 2 small Riverlets that fall in between those Rocks, one on each side, we found 6 or more Families about 35 persons, who gave us a No. of very excellent Fish of two kinds of white Fish,[64] and another *round* green Fish about 14 Inches long   I made them a few Presents and left them,

[62] There is a new handwriting that starts here. It seems that there are two people writing the Journal, who frequently change from one to the other.

[63] You do not see the opening in the solid rock wall until you are within a mile or mile and a half of it. When you enter the opening, the water is very choppy, not exceedingly fast but very rough. The narrowest spot is about a quarter of a mile wide.

[64] *Voyages* inserts "the poisson inconnu."

but all the Men in 15 Canoes followed us—this narrow Channel is 3 Miles long[65] and course N.N.E. then we steered N. 3 Miles, landed at 3 more Families of their people 22 Persons, they were camped close by a midling large River,[66] we got Fish Hares and Partridges from them, and made them Presents of some Articles which pleased them much, they regretted that they had not their goods to exchange with us, they had left them at a Lake that this River runs out of, and where some others of their People set Snares for the Rain Deer, but they said that they would go for them and wait our return which we assured them would be in two Mos at farthest. There was a young lad here who our Indians understood better than any that we had yet seen And was as a Slave with those People, he was asked to come along with us, but he took the first Opp'ty to slip off with himself, and I did not see him afterwards We steered W. 5 miles where we again landed at 2 Families 7 People but we imagine that there were others hid in the wood. we had 2 Doz. of Hares here, and they were about boiling a couple which they gave us also used them the same as I had done the others and left them steering N.W. 4 Miles[67] 9 oClk Camped, one of our Indians killed a grey Crain[68] of us, but the Eskmeaux, who he says are very wicked and will kill us all, that it is but two summers since a great Party of them came up this River and killed a number of his Relations. 2 Indians followed us from the last lodges

WEDNESDAY 8TH.—Embarked at half past 2 A.M. and steered a W. Course.[69] Shortly after we put ashore at 2 lodges of Indians 9 People made them a few Presents without debarking and pushed

[65] It is actually five miles or better, and the direction is northeast, swinging eastward more than north.

[66] *Voyages* adds "which came from the Eastward." This is in the vicinity of the present Fort Good Hope.

[67] According to Mackenzie's reckoning, he traveled thirty-six miles this day. But he had to travel at least sixty-two miles, and if his final directions are anywhere near right, as they could be, he would have traveled about seventy-five miles. This evening it is once more hard to say exactly where he camped.

[68] *Voyages* inserts "Our conductor renewed his complaints, not, as he assured us, from any apprehension." It seems positive that this part of the Journal is a copy in which the copyist missed one or two lines.

[69] Making allowances for any possible campsight, he would be traveling northwest in the main.

off, we did not go far when we observed several Smokes on the North Shore under a Hill, when we approached could see the Indians climbing up the Hill into the wood, the two small Canoes were ahead and spoke to them upon which they returned to their Fires, and we debarked, Many of those People were clothed in Hair[70] Skins but in every thing else they were the same as those we had already seen, tho' we were given to understand that they were a difft. Tribe and called the Hair Indians as Hare (& fish) are their principal support, large animals being very scarce and only Rain Deer and Bever[71] who has an abcess in the Belly and is reduced to a mere Skelton, there were a No. of old women singing and howling there,[72] I distributed a No. of small articles among them which made them quite happy And I charged[73] my Conductor here as he was become very troublesome obliged to watch him night and Day except when upon the water, This fellow had likewise no sooner consented but he repented,[74] alledging that he had not seen much of the River, and that there were more of his Relations close by, who would be willing to accompany us; but we could not believe him as he told us 10 minutes before that we should see no more of their Tribe, so that we made him embark and departed about 3 Hours after a man overtook us in a small Canoe, which we thot. immediately was in Order to facilitate our Conductor to Desert. about 12 oClk we observed a man walking along the N.E. shore the small Canoe made for them and we followed, found 3 men 3 women and 2 children, they had been a Hunting. they had some Rein Deers (meat) which they offered to us, but was so rotten and sunk[75] so abominably that we did not accept of it, they and

[70] Spelled "Hare," in *Voyages*.

[71] *Voyages* inserts "They were twenty-five in number, and among them was a woman." Again a copyist seems to have left out a line in the Journal.

[72] *Voyages* adds "but whether these noises were to operate as a charm for her cure, or merely to amuse and console her, I do not pretend to determine."

[73] The context suggests that this word should be "discharged." *Voyages* has "Here we made an exchange of our guide."

[74] There must be something left out here. *Voyages* has "The man, however, who had agreed to go in his place soon repented . . . ."

[75] Whoever copied this section seems very careless. This word presumably should be "stunk."

the Men that followed us[76] that behind the opposite Island that there was a Manitoe in the Rivers, which swallowed every Person that approached him. It would have taken us half a day to have gone to see this wonder which I did not choose to throw away on an uncertainty, I gave them a Knife and a few awls and departed, one of them embarked in the small Canoe.[77] Our course and distance this Day were W. 28 Miles. W.N.W. 23 Miles W.S.W. 6 Miles W. b N. 5 Miles S.W. 4 Miles,[78] and camped at 8 oclock   the most part of this day was Foggy with frequent showers of small Rain.

THURSDAY 9TH.—Thunder and Rain last Night, our conductor deserted could not find him, embarked one of the others against his will, and took his paddles from the one that remained that he might not follow us, at which he that was in our Canoe got quite enraged, jumped at the Paddle threw it on shore, but we embarked it again and pacified him. at half past 3 left our Campment   in a very short time we saw a Smook on the East shore which we made for. Our Stranger began to Hallow to them in a very strange Manner, he told us that they were not of his Tribe that they were very wicked and would beat us all and pull out our Hair &c. The men waited our arrival, but the women and Children took to the woods, they were only 4 in Number and they began to Harrangue us all at the same time before we debarked, seemingly in a very violent Passion, but our Hunters could not understand what they said— Our Conductor spoke to them and they became quite [quiet?]. I made them presents of Beads, Knives, awls &c.   the women and Children came out of the Wood and met with a similar Treatment, in all they were 15 People, and had a better appearance than any of those we had seen, being healthy and full of Flesh and more

---

[76] Something is missing here. *Voyages* states, "They had also their wonderful stories of danger and terror, as well as their countrymen, whom we had already seen; and we were now informed . . . ."

[77] *Voyages* omits "one of them embarked in the small Canoe."

[78] Again it is very difficult to know where Mackenzie camped this night, but his final direction, "S.W. 4 miles," would suggest a bend in the river about 35 miles below present-day Little Chicago. If this is the case, he would have traveled at the very least 100 and possibly 110 miles. The Journal suggests 66 miles. From what happened on the "9th" I believe my estimations to be correct.

cleanly. Their language was something different, but I believed only in the accent, for they and our Conductor understood one another very well, and the English Chief understood one of them, tho' he could not understand him   Their arms and Utensils differ but little from those I have already described, they have no Iron except very small Pieces that serve them for Knives, which they get from the Eskmeaux,[79] their arrows are made of light wood and have only two Feathers at the End. They had a Bow which is difft. in Shape from theirs, and say they had it from the Eskmeaux who are their neighbours, its of 2 pieces and a very strong Cord of Sinews along the Back of it tied in difft. places to keep it to the Shape which is this. when this Cord gets wet it requires a good Bow String and a strong Arm to draw it, the former must resist the elastic force of the wood and the Cord (I mentd. above) which is very great when it is wet, as it is much contracted,[80] but when it is dry it extends to its common length and is ever then a great support to the Bow. the vessel [in which] they cook their victuals is made of a thin frame of wood, oblong shaped the Bottom fixed in a looc or Notch,[81] same as a Cask. Their Shirts are not cut square at Bottom but tapering to a point from the belt downwards before and behind and come opposite the Knee embellished with a short Fringe   they have another Fringe the same as I have already described, with the addition of a Stone of a grey furmacous[82] Berry of the size and shape of a large Barley Corn, brown clod. and fluted which they bore thro' the middle and run one on each String of the Fringe with which they decorate their shirts by sewing one of them on forming a Demy Circle[83] on the Breast and Back and crossing over both Shoulders   the Sleeves are wide and short, but their Mittens supply this Deficiency, as they are long enough to come over part of the Sleeve, and they wear them—continually

[79] "Esquimeaux Indians," in *Voyages*.
[80] The next lines of the Journal, which speak of the bow when it is dry, are omitted in *Voyages*.
[81] *Voyages* has simply "in a curve."
[82] "Farinaceous berry," in *Voyages*.
[83] "Semicircle," in *Voyages*.

hanging by a cord over their Necks. Their lygens want nothing but waistbands to make them Trowsers, they fasten them with a Cord round the middle so that they are more decent than their Nighbours, Their shoes are sewed to their lygans and garnished on every Seam, one of the Men were dressed in Shirt made of Musgural Skins,[84] the womens dress is the same with the mens, only their Shirts are longer, and have not a Fringe on the Breast, they have a peculiar way of tying the Hair of the Head, viz The Hair of the Temples or fore part of the Skull is tied in the Fashion of two *Queues* and hanging before the Ears, the Hair of the Scalp or Crown is tied in the same manner down to where People commonly tie their Hair at some distance from the Head and hangs in Balance the whole with a Cord about [blank space[85]] wide garnished very neatly with original Hair colod.   some of the Men only dress their Hair in the above Manner, the rest and the women have it hanging loose long or short—Purchased a Couple of very large original Skins[86] from them well dressed—I was surprised to see them have any as I did not think there were any of those Animals in the Country, and they tell us that they are very scarce. they don't know what Beaver is. the men brot. Skeef from them, and Careboof, Collars or Snares, Bows and arrows &c.[87]   we had a Mess of most delicious fish from them, less than a Herring spotted Black and yellow very beautifully had a fin from near the Head to near the Tail, and when stretched was of a Triangular form &[88] varigated the same as the Fish, had a small head and a very sharp set of Teeth. We got the Man who our Indian understood to accompany us which his Predecessor was well pleased at,[89] he says that we will sleep 10 Nights more before[90] we come to the Sea that close by are some of his Relations & that three Nights farther we will meet with

---

84 "Skins of the musk-rat," in *Voyages*.

85 "A thin cord," in *Voyages*.

86 "Large moose skins," in *Voyages*.

87 *Voyages* summarizes most of this list, stating merely, "Our people bought shirts of them, and many curious articles, &c."

88 With the word "varigated," the handwriting very obviously changes.

89 "Which his Predecessor was well pleased at" is omitted in *Voyages*.

90 A word is scratched out in the Journal.

Eskmeaux who formerly made War upon them; but are in Friendship with them at present, he spoke much in derision of the last Indians who we had seen, that they were all like old Women & great Liars &c, which coincides with the opinion I had already entertained of them. As we were pushing off some of my Men fired a Couple of guns load with Powder at the Report of which the Indians were startled, having never heard or seen anything of the kind before, this had like to have prevented our Indian to fulfil his promise, but our Indians made him underst. that what we had done was as a Sign of Friendship & prevailed on him to embark in his own small Canoe tho' he had the offer of a Seat in our, two others who he told us were his Brothers followed us in their Canoes they amused us with Songs of their own & some in Imitation of the Eskmeaux, which seemed to enliven our new Guide so much that he began to dance upon his Breech in his small Canoe & we expected every Moment to see him upset but he was not satisfied with his confined Situation   he paddled up along Side of our Canoe & asked us to embark him (which a little before he had refused) we allowed him & immediately he began to perform an Eskmeaux Dance upon our Canoe when every Person in the Canoe call'd out to him to be quite [quiet?] which he complied with & before he sat down pull'd his *Penis* out of his Breeches laying it on his hand & telling us the Eskmeaux name of it.[91] In short he took much Pains to show us that he knew the Eskmeaux & their Customs   We put on Shore to leave his Canoe, & he informed us the opposite Hill [was where?] the Eskmeaux killed his grandfather three winters ago, we saw a Red Fox & a Sifleur[92] on the Hill, the latter our Conductor's Brother kill'd with his Bow & Arrow   about 4 oClk P.M. we saw a Smoke upon the West Shore traversed & landed   the Natives made a terrible uproar speaking quite loud & running up & down like perfect Madmen   The most of the women & Children had run off with themselves. I was surprised at their appearing in

91 *Voyages* avoids the details here and merely states, "he began to display various indecencies."
92 "Ground hog," in *Voyages*.

such a Passion, as the two small Canoes that followed us had been there some time before us (landed)[93]   I made them Presents of some small Articles but They were fonder of Beads than anything else I gave particularly Blue ones, one of them to whom I had given a Knife asked me to change it for three Branches of Beads which I did to please him, I bought two shirts for my Hunters   they made me a present of arrows & some dry fish which I paid them for.[94] There were 5 families of them but I did not see them all as they kept in their hiding Places. I suppose there might be 40 people Men Women and Children. here I learned that they were called *Diguthe Dinees* or the Quarrelleas,[95] our Conductor like the others wanted to leave us here   he was afraid that we should not come back this way, & besides that the Eskmeaux would perhaps kill us & take their Women from my Men & Indians,[96] & that he was afraid of them too, our Indians told him that we were not afraid & that he need not be, that we certainly should come back this way, he embarked & we pushed off & 8 small Canoes follow'd us, our course to day were S.W. b W. 6 Miles S.W. b S. 30 Miles S.W. 3 Miles W. b S. 12 Miles W. b N. 2 Miles and we encamp'd at 8 oclk on the East Shore.[97] Those Indians told me that from where I met the first of their People this Morning it was not far to go to the Sea over Land on the East Side & from where I found them it was but a short way to go to it to the Westwd. that the land on both sides the River was

[93] *Voyages* adds a considerable amount here, and does not mention the landing of the two small canoes. It states thus: "Perceiving the disorder which our appearance occasioned among these people, we had waited some time before we quitted the canoe; and I have no doubt, if we had been without people to introduce us, that they would have attempted some violence against us; for when the Indians send away their women and children, it is always with a hostile design." Then it goes on with the giving of presents.

[94] "Which I paid them for" is not in *Voyages*.

[95] "*Deguthee Dinees* or the *Quarrellers*," in *Voyages*.

[96] "From my Men & Indians" is left out of *Voyages*.

[97] The river does swing west and south a little through this area. He estimates that he traveled this day fifty-three miles and only two of them in a northerly direction. His account of the "10th" suggests that he spent the evening of the "9th" within a short distance of the lower ramparts. Thus he must have traveled about eighty-five miles, twenty or more of which would have been in a northwesterly direction. He actually camped very little south of the latitude on which he camped the night before.

like a Point.[98] They don't seem to be Thieves, for we cou'd not perceive that they took or wanted to take anything in that way, as soon as we landed they began to dance which differs in no respect from those we had already seen, when this was over they began to jump; and those two seem to be their favorite amusements. In the height of the Day the weather was Sultry but towards the Afternoon became cold, there is a Quantity of wild Flax lying on the ground of last years & the new plant was sprouting up   I observed this no where else.

FRIDAY 10TH.—We embarked at 4 OClk A.M.   not far from our Campment the River narrows between high Rocks & our Course from N.N.W. to S.S.W.[99] say N.W. 4 Miles   here the Banks get low   from the first rapid the Country does not appear so mountainous but the Banks of the River are commonly high and in many Places quite free of Wood & in others well cover'd with Small Trees of the Fir kind & some Birch. we continue our last Course for 2 Miles more, see snowy Mountains ahead, here the land appears low on both Sides except the above mentioned Mountains which are at about 10 Miles distance   the River widens & runs in many Channels amongst Islands[100] some of which are nothing but a bank of Sand & Mud without a Tree, others are covered very thick with a kind of white Spruce[101] & larger Trees than any we have seen this 10 Days. the Banks of those which are abt. 6 ft above the Surface of the Water shews a face of solid Ice—intermix'd with a Black Earth & as the heat of the Sun melts this Ice the Trees are continually tumbling in the River.[102] we were much at a loss what

[98] This story could have hardly been true. However, going northeast or north from where the Mackenzie River swings in a southwesterly direction it is not too far across land to the sea or to a lake and river system flowing into the sea.

[99] "From N.N.W." to "S.S.W." is left out of *Voyages*, in spite of the fact that the Journal is fairly accurate here.

[100] Of course Mackenzie has entered the delta here. He has only mentioned six miles when he has really traveled at least twenty or twenty-five. From the morning of the "10th" it becomes increasingly difficult to follow Mackenzie's descriptions and mileages until Tuesday, July 21, when he is out of the delta region and back to his camp of the "9th."

[101] *Voyages* calls this "spruce fir"; no "white" is mentioned.

[102] This is still a good word picture of the delta region as someone rounding Point Separation sees it today.

Channel out of some hundred to take   our Conductor[103] was for taking the Eastmost, on account as he said that the Eskmeaux were close by on that Road, but I determined upon taking the middle as it was a large piece of water and running N. & S.[104] I hoped to get an Observation,[105] and that we would always go to the Eastward afterwards; our course W. b N. 6 Miles N.W. b W.   the snowy mountains W. b S. from us and running to the Northward as far as we could see, the Indians say they are part of the chain of Mountains we came to the 3d. Inst.   at Noon I got an Observation which gave me 67° 47′ North lat. which is further North than I expected, according to the course I kept, but the difference is partly[106] owing to the variation of the Compass which is more Easterly than that I thought. I am much at a loss here how to act being certain that my going further in this Direction will not answer the Purpose of which the Voyage was intended,[107] as it is evident these waters must empty themselves into the Northern Ocean,[108] but as it is my Opinion as well as my mens, that as we would not be able to get to the Athabasca this Season by Water, not but the time would permit but our want of Provision would prevent us, therefore I determined to go to the discharge of those waters, as it would satisfy Peoples curiosity tho' not their Intentions—My new conductor is quite discouraged and tired of his Situation, says he never saw the Billhully Toe[109] (which means lake) that he only was at Eskmeaux lake which is not far off, that he never had been at it this way, that he went to it overland from where we found him and to where the Eskmeaux pass the Summer, all this—discouraged my Hunters and am confident were it in their power would leave me, as they are

103 With "Conductor" the handwriting changes once more.

104 Amazingly enough this direction is correct today, 1965. One must always remember that a delta is always changing: that which is true one year need not be true the next. The river bed becomes more variable the closer one gets to the ocean.

105 "I hoped to get an Observation" is left out of *Voyages*.

106 "Partly" is left out in *Voyages*, thus blaming all the difference on the compass.

107 The whole section starting "I am much at a loss" down to "intended" is left out of *Voyages*.

108 The "Hyperborean Sea," in *Voyages*.

109 *"Benahulla Toe*, or White Man's Lake," in *Voyages*.

quite disquieted with the voyage. I satisfied them a little by telling them I would go on but 7 days more, and that if I did not come to the sea in that time that I should return, and my scarcity of Provisions will make me fulfil this promise, whether I will or not. Our last Course 32 miles, the Current is stronger than could be expected in such a low country N.N.W. 4 Miles N.W. 3 Miles N.E. 2 Miles N.W. b W. 3 Miles N.E. 2 miles   at half past 8 P.M. camped[110] close by where [there were] three old Campments since the Ice broke up. Our Conductor says they were Eskmeaux   we saw many wild fowl today. The Natives who followed us Yesterday parted with us close by our campment this morning.

SATURDAY 11TH.—I sat up last Night to observe at what time the Sun would set, but found that he did not set at all   at half past 12 I called upon one of the men to see what he never saw before.[111] We took our rest till ¾ past 3 when we embarked steering about N.W. the River very serpenting   about 7 oClk see a ridge of high land[112] on the N.E. side. Our conductor says the Road [to which] he wanted to bring us runs along this highland.[113] At 12 oClock we landed at a plain where we observed some of the Natives had been lately, I counted the places of upwards of 30 Fires and some of the men went farther where they say [are] many more,[114] they must have been here some time, tho' they had made no Huts, there are a great No. of Poles stuck in the ground in the River to which they fastened their Nets, and there seems to be an excellent Fishery

110 If by "Our last Course 32 miles," which appears directly above, Mackenzie meant thirty-two miles north from Point Separation, then it is possible he camped just above what is today known as the R.C.M.P. Fish Camp. The site would agree with the direction he took the next morning and also the morning's complaint that the river was "very serpenting." If he did camp here, he traveled this day about seventy or seventy-five miles, which is about right considering the sluggish current once one reaches the delta.

111 *Voyages* adds "when, on seeing the sun so high, he thought it was a signal to embark, and he began to call the rest of his companions, who would scarcely be persuaded by me, that the sun had not decended nearer to the horizon, and that it was not but a short time past midnight."

112 Today the Caribou Hills.

113 "Our conductor says the Road he wanted to bring us runs along this highland" is left out of *Voyages*.

114 *Voyages* has "saw as many more," thus distorting the meaning of the Journal.

here, we saw many jump out of the water, one of which fell into our Canoe, which was about 10 inches long and round, we found scattered round their fire places pieces of whale bone, very thick Leather[115] which had been used, pieces of the Frames of their Canoes &c.   We could observe where they had spilt Train Oil in several places, close by was a Spruce Tree branched up to the Top as May pole. The weather Cloudy and disaggreable cold, from this place for about 4 Miles the River is wide,[116] then it runs in narrow winding Channels amongst low Islands with hardly a tree, and the only ones are Willows, very small and low, at 4 oClock we landed at 3 Huts or Houses, the ground plot of them is an oval square about 15 feet long 10 feet wide in the middle and about 8 feet at each End, the half[117] of this is dug about a foot below the surface of the Earth, and covered over with Willow Branches,[118] and I suppose serves for a Bed for all the Family, the Middle of the other part is dug a foot deeper in the ground, and is the only part of the House where a Person can stand upright,[119] the space on each side of this is upon a level with the former one, of which is covered in the same manner, and the other is the Fire place, of which they don't make much tho'   close by the Wall the latter is not burnt, the Door is in the middle of the End of the House, its about 2½ feet by 2, and has a covered way 5 feet long, to go into the House you must creep on all fours, there is a Hole 18 Inches Square on the Top of the House, which lets in the light. I suppose some times serves there as a Door and lets out the Smoak, tho' it is not over the Fire place, what is under ground of the House is lined

115 "Thick burned leather," in *Voyages*.

116 This sounds like the spot some five miles west and two or three miles south of present-day Tununuk, where the middle channel branches. However, this location would be about sixty-five miles from where I placed his camp the night before, which distance, in eight hours paddling, is not likely to be correct. Thus there must have been at that time a similar spot not so far out in the delta.

117 "Whole" instead of "half," in *Voyages*.

118 The Eskimo still uses willow branches for his floor—his entire floor—in the delta region.

119 The sentence following the word "upright" reads thus in *Voyages*: "One side of it is covered, as has been already described, and the other is the hearth or fire-place, of which, however, they do not make much use."

with split wood, 6 or 8 stumps of small Trees drove in the ground, the Root upwards upon which are laid Cross pieces, supports the whole Building.[120] The Top of the House or Roof is a long square 10 feet by 6 ft, the whole is made of drift wood covered with Branches and dry grass, over which is laid Earth a foot deep, along side of each of these Houses are two or three Square Holes dug 2 feet deep in the ground, and covered over with split wood and Earth, except in the middle, and I suppose those are Cellars wherein they keep their winter's provisions. In and about the Houses we found Sledge runners &c. Bones, pieces of whale bone, Bark of Poplar cut round which they use as Cask[121] to Buoy up their Nets to which it is fastened with a piece of Whale Bone &c. and before each Hut are a Number of Stumps of Trees (drift wood) stuck in the ground, upon which it appeared they hung their Fish,[122] we continued our Route, and at 8 oClk we camped, I suppose our Course about N.W., and allowing for the windings that we came 54 Miles.[123] All day we expected that we should meet with some of the Natives, on several Islands we saw the print of their Feet on the sand, running after wild Fowls, and by appearance not 3 Days ago. Frequent showers of Rain this afternoon, the weather raw and very disaggreeable   Saw a black Fox, not a tree to be seen, except a few willows which are not above 3 feet high. Our Hunters are in a very bad Humour, our guide has been telling them that will see the lake tomorrow, and that it is not a Lake I *ans dessan* that it is not a small one,[124] that he nor his relations know nothing about it, except that part of it which is opposite to, and not far from their land, only the Eskmeaux live about it that they kill a large Fish in it which they eat, and from the Description must be the Whale, and a great many white Bears, and another large animal, but our Hunters could not understand the Description he

[120] "Support the roof of the building," in *Voyages*.
[121] "Cork" instead of "Cask," in *Voyages*.
[122] *Voyages* adds "to dry."
[123] According to this mileage, Mackenzie was still ten to fifteen miles south and west of Tununuk.
[124] *Voyages* leaves out "and that it is not a Lake I *ans dessan* that it is not a small one."

gave of it, that they have very large Canoes in which 4 or 5 Families embark. Gave one of my Capels to the English Chief, and an Original Skin to our guide.[125]

SUNDAY 12TH.—Rained hard last night and till 7 o'Clock[126] this morning, the weather cold, we embarked, our course winding as yesterday. the wind N.N.W. hardly a shrub to be seen,[127] at 10 oClock A.M. landed at 4 Huts, same as we saw yesterday, close by the land is high and covered with short grass and many Plants, which are in Blossom, and has a beautiful appearance, tho' an odd contrast, the Hills covered with Flowers and Verdure, and the vallies full of Ice and Snow, the Earth is not thawed above 4 Inches from the Surface, below is a solid Body of Ice. the Soil is a yellow clay mixed with Stone.[128] those Huts appear to have been inhabited last winter, the Natives had lately been here, the Beach was covered with the Track of their feet, many of their Runners and Bars of their Sledges by the Houses, and laid together as if they intended to come and take them again. pieces of Net made of Sinews and some of the Bark of the Willow Tree. The Thread of the former was plated and must take them much time and pains to plate such a length of Cord, a square Stone Kettle, could contain about 2 galls., its very surprising how they could have dug it out, the Bottom is flat, small pieces of Flint fixed into a piece of wood (we supposed a knife, several wooden Dishes and Troughs, Stern and part of the Keel of a large Canoe   very thick Leather we thot. the covering of the Canoe, many bones of large size Fish and part of two big Heads, we don't know of what animal, I suppose the Sea Horses! After we had satisfied our Curiosity here,

125 *Voyages* changes this sentence considerably: "However, to reconcile the English Chief to the necessary continuance in my service, I presented him with one of my capots or travelling coats; at the same time to satisfy the guide, and keep him, if possible, in good humor, I gave him a skin of the moose-deer, which, in his opinion, was a valuable present."

126 *Voyages* has "till two in the morning" though the Journal clearly states that it was seven.

127 At this point he seems to be above the tree line, which could have been further south then than now.

128 The hills, valleys, and soil suggest some part of present-day Richard's Island though he would have had to go north and slightly east to get there.

we embarked, tho' we did not know what course to steer, our guide being as ignorant in this country as any of ourselves, this appeared to be the Entrance of the Lake, tho' the current was yet very strong and set West, and we went with it for a high point about 8 Miles distant, which we took to be an Island separate from the plain, where we had last landed, but we found it to be joined by a Neck of low land, I had an observation which gave me 69° 1′ N.L.[129]

from the above mentioned Course we continued the same Course for the Westermost part of a high Island and the most Western land in [sight[130]] distant 15 miles   the Lake was quite open to us to the Westward and out of the Canal of the River not above 4 feet water, and in some places no more than one. the shallowness of the water makes it impossible to *Cost*[131] it to the Westward, at 5 o'Clock we came to the Island and during the last 15 Miles 5 feet was the deepest Water, from here we could see the Lake covered with Ice at about 2 Leagues distance and no land ahead, so that we stopped by the Ice ahead and the shallowness of the water along shore, and we landed at the limit of our Travels in this Direction[132] as soon as our Tents were pitched I ordered the men and Indians to set Nets, and I went with the English Chief to the highest part of the Island from which we could see the Ice in a whole Body extending from the S.W. by Compass to the Eastward as far as we could see—To the Southward we could just perceive a chain of Mountains extending farther to the North than the Edge of the Ice   distant upwards of 20 leagues to the Eastward are great many Islands,[133] in our Walk saw many white Partridges (now Brown)

[129] If this reading is correct, it would place him almost directly west and a mile or two north of Tununuk.

[130] A word is scratched out in the Journal. *Voyages* has "the Westernmost land in sight, at the distance of fifteen miles."

[131] "Coast," in *Voyages*.

[132] Mackenzie's estimation of his North Latitude on the whole was rather accurate. If his previous reading of "69° 1′ N. L." (see footnote 128) was correct and his last two distances of eight and fifteen miles in a westerly direction were approximately correct, it would place him several miles north of Tununuk, about halfway between Tununuk and present-day Ellice Island.

[133] These could be the hills on Richard Island or other small islands which today make up part of the delta. Ellice Island is flat and only four to five feet high, so would not be seen.

very beautiful Plovers, the nest of one of those I found with 4 Eggs, white Owls, and also the grave of one of the Natives, by which lay a Bow double Paddle spear &c. The Indians tell me that they landed upon a small Island, about 4 leagues from here, where they saw the Tracks of 2 Men quite fresh. and that they had taken up[134] *a Cache* of Train Oil, many Bones of white Bears close by where the Oil was hid, the wind is so high that we can't[135] visit our Nets. My men express much sorrow that they are obliged to return without seeing the sea, in which I believe them sincere for we marched exceeding hard coming down the River, and I never heard them grumble; but on the contrary in good Spirits, and in hope every day that the next would bring them to the *Mer d' Ouest*, and declare themselves now and at any time ready to go with me whenever I choose to lead them. Saw several large white gatts,[136] another large Bird, the Back and upper parts of the wings Brown, the Belly and under part of the wings white.

MONDAY 13TH.—Soon after we went to Bed last Night,[137] some of them were obliged to get up and move the Baggage on account of the water rising. at 8 o'Clock A.M. we got up, the Men and Indians went to their Nets. fine calm weather, could not find one of them, the Current and wind drove it from where they had set it. In the other caught 7 large white Fish,[138] which are not good, a large white Fish of the small Kind[139] which is excellent Another Fish about the size of an Herring, which none of us know, except the English Chief, who says, they are very plentiful at Hudson's Bay—Towards Noon Blows hard from the Westward, have an Observation which gives 69° 14'[140] N. Lat. by a Meridian variation

134 *Voyages* has "found a secrete store" but does not mention their taking up the "*Cache*."

135 *Voyages* says it was "impractical" to visit the nets.

136 *Voyages* has "white gulls"; however, the Journal clearly has "gatts." The letter *t* is crossed in both cases and the *a* is closed.

137 *Voyages* inserts "if I may use that expression, in a country where the sun never sinks beneath the horizon."

138 "We caught seven poissons inconnus," in *Voyages*.

139 "Of the small Kind" is left out of *Voyages*.

140 This reading would suggest Mackenzie was about fifteen miles west and fifteen miles north of Tununuk.

of the Compass 36 Degrees Easterly, this afternoon I ascended the Hill, I could not perceive the Ice had moved,—notwithstanding the force of the wind, can just distinguish 2 small Islands in the Ice to the N.W. by Compass.[141] I gave a new Nett to my Men to mount as we must live upon Fish whenever we can catch any our Provisions being reduced to 6 ps. say 510 lbs. among 15 people, which without any other supply would not last us above 12 Days, one of the young Indians found our Net with 3 of the largest kind of white Fish

TUESDAY 14TH.—Blew very hard from the N.W. since Yesterday Evening, having sat up till 3 o'Clock this morning, I was late a getting up. About 8 one of my men saw a great many animals in the water which he took first to be Pieces of Ice,[142] he waken'd all the others to see this sight. I immediately knew them to be whales, and ordered the Men, to put the Canoe in the water, we embarked to pursue them[143] but could not come up with any of them, the weather being Foggy prevented our going far after them. Our Conductor says it is such Fish as those the Eskmeaux kill, some of them bigger than our Canoe, what appeared out of the water of those Fish was quite white, but they appeared too large for Porposes. About 12 o'Clock the Fog cleared away and as I had a Curiosity of seeing the Ice, I ordered my men to load the Canoe, we embarked, and the Indians followed us, we were not above an hour on the water, when the Wind of a sudden rose from the N.E. and obliged us to veer about, the Fog prevented our seeing[144] how near we had been to the Ice & we hardly see the Island we came from   we hoisted our Sail tho' the Wind was very near   the Swell augmented & it was as much as two men could do to bale out the Water   in short we ran a great risk & never was happier than when we got safe to Land, the Indians were still in more danger

141 Most likely Garry Island and Kendall Island.

142 *Voyages* inserts "About nine, however, I was awakened to resolve the doubts which had taken place respecting this extraordinary appearance." It leaves out the phrase "he waken'd all the others to see this sight."

143 *Voyages* adds that it was an "unreflecting enterprise" and that the tail could have "dashed the canoe to pieces."

144 The handwriting changes.

than we but very lucky for them they had been much farther to windward than we the Swell in a manner drove them on Shore the Canoes full of water, in all likelihood had they been loaded we should never have seen them, as I did not chuse to run any more risk this way to satisfy my Curiosity, as soon as the men had rested we continued going on along the Island which screened us from the wind, as I intend to lose two or three Days to search for the Natives among the Islands, from whom perhaps I might get some interesting Intelligence tho' my Conductor assured me they are a very un-accotable set of Beings[145] & most likely he says we wou'd see some of them if we went by the Road he wanted us to come down. At 8 oClk we camped upon the East end of the Island. (wh I called whale Island) it's abt 7 Leagues long E. and W. by Compass not above half a Mile wide.[146] we saw several Red Foxes one of which a Young man kill'd. There are 5 or 6 old Huts on this Point, we set our Nets one of them in 5 fathom water, Current Setting at E.[147] by Compass This morning I fixed[148] a Post close by or Campmt. on which I engraved the latitude of the Place. My own Name & the Number of Men with me & the time we had been here.

WEDNESDAY 15TH.—I happen'd to wake about 4 this Morning I was surprised to ["find" crossed out] observe the water had come under our Baggage as the wind had not changed nor blew harder than when we went to Bed, I waken'd my men to move the Baggage &c.[149] we were all of opinion that it was the Tide as we had ob-served at the other End of the Island that the water rose & fell but we thot that this had been occasioned by the Wind it continued to rise till about 6, but I could not exactly know the time as the

145 A "shy and inaccessible people," in *Voyages*.

146 Very few maps of the scores I have gone through ever pinpoint Whale Island. Some merely write the name on the outer edge of the delta and allow your imagina-tion to place it on any island you want; others do not even list the name. There is one map, however, that of McLure, 1850, which places Whale Island halfway between Ellice Island and Richard Island. Today it would be part of the delta region, but according to McLure's map it was then, in 1850, on the outside of the delta as Kendall Island is today.

147 "North-East," in *Voyages*.

148 "I ordered a post to be erected," in *Voyages*.

149 From "I awakened" to "baggage &c." is left out of *Voyages*.

wind then began to blow very violently   however to put it out of doubt I intend to remain here till next morning, indeed if I were willing to go off now the wind would prevent me. visited our Nets caught but 8 Fish. had an Observation at Noon 69° 7 North towards the Evening the wind augmented, and the Weather cold, the Indians kill'd 2 Swan.

THURSDAY 15TH.[150]—Rain'd till 7 oclk this Morning the weather Cold & very disagreeable, as near as the inconstancy of the weather would allow me to observe the Tide rises 16 or 18 Inches, we embarked & steered under sail among the Islands in hopes of meeting with some of the Natives but all to no purpose, Our Conductor says they are gone to where they fish for whales, & kill Rein Deer opposite to his Land, & that he & his Relations sees them there every year that the water is very deep there & that we shall see none of them, without it be at a small River that falls into the grand River from the Eastward, & a good way from here by the way that he wanted us to come down   as we give up hopes of seeing any of the Natives here abouts[151] we made for the river & stemm'd the Currt. at 2 oClk P.M.   the water was quite shallow every where we passed   could always find bottom with a Paddle   at 7 oClk P.M. we camp'd set our Nets,[152] the Indians kill'd 2 geese, 2 Cranes & a white Owl   we find a great change in the Weather since we entered the River being very agreable but we are much tormented by Musquittoes in consequence

FRIDAY 17TH.—took up our Nets caught but 6 Fish   embark'd at 4 oClk A.M.   passed several[153] Campments which appeared not to have been long ago. landed upon a round small Island[154] close to the Easter Shore on top of which were many graves, Frame of a Small Canoe, Paddles sledges, Dishes, Troughs, &c. laying about which makes it evident that the living make no use of the Property

[150] *Voyages* has the correct date, the 16th.

[151] From "by the way" to "here abouts" is omitted in *Voyages*.

[152] We have really no way of knowing where he camped this night, perhaps on Richard Island.

[153] "Four encampments," in *Voyages*.

[154] This could be Tununuk, but why does he not speak of the east channel which branches off here for present-day Port Brabant (Tuktoyaktuk)?

of those that die,[155] there was not any of the skins that covered the Canoe remaining, I suppose it must have been eat up by wild animals. The Frame was put together with whalebone sewed in some parts & tied in others the whole entire. The Sledges are from 4 to 8 ft. long the Bars upwards of 2 ft. long and the runners are each 2 Inches thick & 9 Inches deep, the Curve[156] is 2½ ft. high & of two pieces sewed with whale Bone. to this & their other[157] thin Spars of wood which come to the same height & fixed in runner by means of Mortices, are sewed two thin Broad Bars length ways at a little distance from one another, these Frames are fixed together with 3 or 4 Bars tied tight down upon the Runners, upon the lower edge of the latter are peg'd with wooden Pegs Pieces of Samall Bone or Horn, that they may slide the easier, they draw them by Shafts,[158] tho' I only saw one pr. among several Sledges, about half past 1. we came opposite to the first *Epinettes*[159] those upon the Main Land[160] are but few & very small, them that are upon the Island are larger and grow quite close to one another, but only in Patches   indeed it is surprising that their should be any Wood at all in a Country where the ground does not thaw 6[161] Inches from the Surface—Camp'd at 7 o Clock[162] P.M. fine weather saw many wild Fowl to-day with their Young ones, but they were so shy that we cou'd not approach them. The Indians kill'd 2 Grey Cranes & a Grey Brant, 2 of them walk'd the most

155 *Voyages* forms no conclusions but states merely, "We found the frame of a small canoe, with various dishes, troughs, and other utensils, which had been the living property of those who could not use them no more, and form the ordinary accompaniments of their last abodes."

156 "Prow," in *Voyages.*

157 "To three other" instead of "to this & their other," in *Voyages.*

158 *Voyages* adds "which I imagine are applied to any particular sledge as they are wanted."

159 "Spruce-tree," in *Voyages. Epinettes* is French for North American fir trees. Mackenzie is coming back below the tree line once more. Today this would be about halfway between Tununuk and Reindeer Depot, though the tree line seems to be constantly moving north. We were carrying an old map and there were odd spruce trees well above the tree line on the map.

160 This would suggest he is in the East Channel, but he never says explicitly that he is there.

161 *Voyages* uses "five inches" though the Journal very clearly states six.

162 Again we have little idea of where he camped.

of the Day in hopes of seeing & killing Rein Deer, they were disappointed saw only a few Tracks. I ascended the high land from
which I had a delightful prospect of the River, Hundreds of Streams
meandring thro' Islands some cover'd with wood & others with
Grass, the opposite Mountains about 40 Miles distant,[163] the inland
view was neither so extensive nor so agreeable, being terminated by
Black Barren Hills at no great Distance, between which are small
Lakes or Ponds, & the country around—cover'd with Tuffs of
Moss not a Tree to be seen.   all along the Hill are a kind of Fence
made with Branches when the Natives had set Snares to catch
white Partridges[164]

SATURDAY 18TH.—took up our Nets without a single Fish   got
underway at 8 oClk A.M.[165] the weather fine & clear   pass a No. of
Campments the print of the Natives feet on the Sand, so that it
can't be a long time since they have been (above 6 Inches from the
Surface Cam'd at 7 oClk P.M.   fine weather saw many wild Fowl
to-day with their Young Ones, but they were so shy)[166] here   we
hope to see some of them at the River at which our Conductors
says there always are some, which we will pass tomorrow[167]   we
observed a Number of Trees Branched to the Top in several Places,
it seems the Natives does this close by their winter Quarters to
direct one another, Our Hunters kill's 2 Rein Deer to Day the first
& only large animal which we have seen since we have been in this
River, & is a very seasonable Supply. Our Pemmican has been
mouldy this long time past but in our Situation we must eat it &

---

[163] This would suggest he may have camped near present-day Reindeer Depot.
It is only about a fifteen-minute hike from the river to the "high land" or top of the
Caribou Hills. The scene of the delta from here is magnificent, and of course to the
east are the treeless barrens, which are not really barren, for they do support reindeer
today. From this vantage point the mountains behind Aklavik, on the west side
of the delta, are easily seen and are "about 40 miles distant."

[164] On our 1965 excursion we saw an Eskimo boy coming off the same hills with
one hand full of partridges and with a gun in the other.

[165] "Three o'clock," in *Voyages*.

[166] The three lines in brackets are crossed out in the Journal, for they are dupli-
cates of the preceeding page copied verbatim and do not belong here. This mistake
would seem to me to be additional proof that this is not Mackenzie's original draft
but a copy made by several hands, his own being one.

[167] "Which we will pass tomorrow" is left out of *Voyages*.

not loose a particle of it, we did not lose above 3 Hours time going for the above Animals as they were kill'd on the declivity of the Land in sight of our Canoe[168] In the Vallies and low land close by the River & facing the Sun are plenty of Cranberries, can gather those of last Year & those of this upon the same Shrub, another Berry of a whitish Yellow Colour resembling a Rasberry Pathagominan[169] & very well tasted, & Number of Plants & Herbs which I am not acquainted with. The weather became cold towards The afternoon, appearance of Rain Camp'd at 7 oclk P.M.[170] The Young Indian kill'd 8 geese—the most part of the Day I walked with the English Chief and found it very disagreeable & fatiguing tho' the Country is so high its nothing but a Morass except the tops of a few Barren Hills. I had my Hanger in my Hand & tried frequently if any part of the ground thaw'd but cou'd never make it enter above 6 or 8 Ins   The face of this high land to the River is in some Places Rocky in other Places Sandy mixt with Stone & clay, in this are Veins of Red Earth wch the Natives bedaub themselves with

SUNDAY 19TH.—Rain'd & blew a hard North Wind till 8 this Morning   when we got up we found that our Conductor had ran off with himself, I was surprised at the fellow's honesty, he left a Skin I had given him to cover himself, & went off in his Shirt, tho' the weather is very cold, I enquired of the Indians if they had given him any reason to desert, or if they had perceived that he wish'd to leave us, they assur'd me that they had given him no reason, that some time ago he was saying to them that he was afraid we should take him away as a slave, and that they believed he was frightened Yesterday when he saw them kill the two Rein Deer with so little Trouble. towards the Afternoon the weather became fine & clear, we saw vast flocks of geese with their Young, the Hunters kill'd 22

---

168 From "we did not" to "our Canoe" is omitted in *Voyages*.

169 "Pathagominan" is not in *Voyages*. It is quite likely what is known today as the salmon berry.

170 Again one is at a loss to know where Mackenzie camped this evening, but it seems obvious he is following the mainland up the east channel.

& the Men 2[171]   they have cast their feathers & can't fly and are of a very small kind not near so large as those about Athabasca. At 8 oClock we camp'd close by on Indian Campment where were pieces of whalebone, Rein Deer Horn, & they had work'd Wood here.[172]

[173]MONDAY 20TH.—Embarked at 3 this morning, cloudy weather, small Rain, aft wind, about 12 the rain pour'd down upon us plentifully, and obliged us to camp at 2 P.M.   we saw great Numbers of Fowl, we killed 2 geese and 4 Swans, the Indians 8 geese 4 Brants;[174] we would have killed many more had the weather been favorable, passed the River[175] where we expected to have met with some of the Natives without seeing any Signs of their being there lately; saw none of their campments since 10 oClock A.M.   here abouts the land is not high close by the river, the Hills at a distance are covered with Epinette and small Birch to their Tops

TUESDAY 21ST.—Embarked this morning at half past 1 oClock, the weather disagreeable cold, Wind S.W. at 10 oClock got out from among the Islands, where the River is but one Channel,[176] we find the Current so strong here that we are obliged to Tow our Canoe with a line, the land on both sides [of] the River is high and almost perpendicular to the River, the Beach under this is not very wide and covered with grey Free stone which falls from the Precipice, we make much more way with the line than the Paddle. The men in the Canoe spells 2 of those on shore every two Hours, so that there is always one of them that goes in his turn every 4 Hours without resting, by this way we lose little or no time to rest, but it

171 "& the men 2" is left out in *Voyages*.

172 *Voyages* explains, "working wood into arms, utensils &c." Again I do not know where he camped except that he must be still in Eskimo country because of the whalebone. If so, he is still on the delta.

173 The handwriting changes.

174 In telling the numbers of fowl killed, *Voyages* states merely "killed among us fifteen geese and four swans."

175 Most likely the river flowing into the east channel from Campbell Lake.

176 He has once more passed Point Separation going upstream and we can follow him much better.

is very hard duty,[177] at ½ past 8 o'Clock P.M. we landed at our Campment of the 9TH Instant, about 2 hours after 11 of the Natives joined us,[178] they were camped further up the River, there were 4 or 5 of those we had not seen before, the Brother of our Conductor enquired after him, we informed him of what happened, but it did not satisfy him or any of those along with him, they all appeared anxious, and each made his harrangue upon the Occasion, but our Indians said they did not understand them, that they say they spoke ill, his Brother asked me for some blue Beads, and then that he would believe what we said, I paid no attention to him, ordered one of my men to deliver to him his Brother's Bow and arrow which he had left with us, all hands were pulling their Fusils in order after Yesterday's Rain, the Natives wanted much to know what we were going to do with them, we shewed them a piece of Meat,[179] and told them it was to kill such as that, and that we had no intention of killing them, they begged that we should not fire now, I made the English Chief ask them some questions which they did not, or pretended not, to understand, so that we could not learn anything from them. My men and Indians went to rest, I sat up to observe the Natives motions, they wanted to know why I went not to Bed, and being busy writing this they had a Curiosity to see and know the meaning of it, about 12 oclock I saw four of their women coming along the shore, as soon as their friends perceived them, two young men ran to meet them made two of them return, who I suppose were young and the two others were very old. accompanied them to our Fire, remained half an hour and went back again, the men shortly after made a small Fire for themselves, and slept round it like a parcel of whelps, having neither Skins nor Robes to cover themselves, tho' the weather is cold, my men had put their Kettle full of meat on the Fire, I was obliged to prevent the Natives several times from taking it, this was the first Instance I saw of

---

[177] *Voyages* leaves out a considerable amount here, stating only, "The men in the canoe relieved two of those on shore every two hours, so that it was very hard and fatiguing duty, but it saves a great deal of that time which was so precious to us."

[178] "In about an hour after our arrival, we were joined by eleven," in *Voyages*.

[179] *Voyages* adds "and a goose."

any of them wishing to take what was not their own; but I suppose they think provision should be common Property—among all People. This is the first time I saw the sun set since I camped here before as it did not ["fall" scratched out] before [or] come near our Horizon, except it was last Night the weather being so cloudy that I could not see it, the water has fallen at this place upwards of 3 feet since we passed down.

WEDNESDAY 23D. [22D?]—We began our March half past 3 this morning, the men on the lines   I walked with the Indians to their Huts which were further off than what expected, we took 3 Hours hard walking to get to them, passed a narrow deep River in our way, at the Entrance of which the Natives had Nets set, they had hid their Effects and young Women in the wood, as we saw but few of the former and none of the latter, They have a large Hut built with Drift wood upon the Declivity of the Beach and dug in the Inside to a level, at each end are two stout Forks whereon is laid a strong Ridge Pole, which supports the whole structure, its covered Epinelle[180] Bark to keep out the Rain—Number of Spars at difft. hts. from one end of the Hut to the other covered with Fish, split open to dry, they make Fires in difft. parts of the House that the fish may dry the sooner: They have Rails on the Outside of the House which are likewise covered with Fish, but fresher than those in the Hut. they appear very careful of the Roes or sperme of the Fish which they dry in like manner, we got as many Fish from them as we chose to embark, for which I gave them Beads, as they were fonder of them than of any thing I possessed, tho' I did not observe they had any of them. Iron they put little value in. During 2 Hours that I remained here I kept the English Chief continually questioning them—the result of which is as follows that their Nation or Tribe is very numerous, that the Eskmeaux are always at variance with them, that they kill their Relations when they find them weak notwithstanding they promise to be always Friends, they of late have shown their Treachery by Butchering some of their People in proof of which some of the Relations of those de-

180 The word should probably be "Epinette."

ceased shewed us that they had [181] cut of [off?] their Hair upon the occasion, & that they are determined not to believe the Eskmeaux anymore; that they will collect all their Friends to go to revenge the Death of their Friends. That a strong Party of the Eskmeaux comes up this River in their large Canoes in search of Flint Stones to point their Spears and Arrows, that they were now at their Lakes due East[182] from where we are now, that the distance is not great over land where they kill the Rein Deer & that they will begin soon to kill big fish for their winter Stock, that they know nothing about the Lake in the Direction we were in. To the Eastwd. and the Westd. the Ice breaks up but soon freezes again. The Eskmeaux saw large Canoes full of white men to the Westward 8 or 10 Winters since, from whom they got Iron of which they exchang'd part with them for leather. where the big Canoes came to they call *Belan howlay Tock*.[183] (white Mens lake)

That the Eskmeaux dress like them wear their Hair short, have two holes one on each Side of the Mouth in a line with the under lip in which they stick long Beads which they find in their Lakes, their Bows differ from theirs they make use of Slings to throw stones at their Enemies, at which they are very dextrous.

They likewise informed us that we should not see any more of their Relations, that they had all left the River to go & kill Rein Deer for their winters Provision, & that they intended to do the same in a few Days; that Rein Deers, Bears, Carcajeaux,[184] Martin, Foxes, Hares & white Buffaloe, are the only quadrupedes upon their lands, the latter are only to be met with in the mountains to the Westward. went with the line all Day except 2 Hours Sailing, we camp'd at 8 oClock[185] from where we started this Morning, the

181 The handwriting changes.

182 This would have to be northeast to get to Eskimo Lake.

183 "*Belhoullay Toe*," in *Voyages*. This lake would be far to the northwest. Just how far I would not like to guess. It is possible that an enterprising Englishman had made it through the Bering Straits. It would be far more likely a Russian vessel of some sort in the vicinity of present-day Point Barrow perhaps.

184 "Wolvereens," in *Voyages*.

185 We have no way of knowing the campsite except that the following evening they camp at their "campment of the 8th." It seems as though it took them just about two days to make the distance upstream that they made in one day downstream.

View from the top of Granite Hill, where Mackenzie climbed on June 12
to look for a break in the ice on the lake.

Looking out of the north channel of the Mackenzie River into Great Slave Lake, where Mackenzie was "at a loss what course to take" on June 29.

The "high hill" which Mackenzie climbed on July 3.

The mountains signifying the entrance of Great Bear River, seen by
Mackenzie on July 5.

The Ramparts of July 7, which Mackenzie found much less dangerous than the Indians had led him to expect.

A bear swimming in the Lower Ramparts.

Mary and Pat with our canoe near the Arctic Circle.

The Mackenzie delta, where Mackenzie was July 10–20.

Banks of the River are well covered with Small wood, Epinette, Birch & Willows we found it very warm travelling—

THURSDAY 23D.—got underway at 5 A.M. very difficult walking along the Beach   passed several Places where the Natives had Camp'd, & set nets, since we had passed down passed a small River at 5 oclock, here our Indians put on Shore to camp   we passed, which displeased them very much. they were quite fatigued. Camp'd at 8 oClk at our Campment of the 8TH. Inst   the weather very fine to Day all Day upon the line, our Hunters join'd us at 10 oClock very sulky, we did not touch our Provisions these 6 Days past in which time we have eat 2 Rein Deer, 4 Swans, 45 Geese, 1 Brant[186] a great many Fish, among 10 men 4 women & a Boy,[187] I always found North Men bless'd with good appetites. but nothing equal to what ours are, & has been since we enter'd the River, I wou'd have thot. it gluttoness in any Men, did I not find that my own appetite has augmented in proportion to theirs.[188]

FRIDAY 24TH.—We embark'd at 5 oClk but shortly after we were obliged to have recourse to our line, the Stream being too strong to stem it with Paddles   at 8 we passed a small River at each Side of wch the Natives & Eskmeaux get Flint, the Bank is a steep high soft Rock varigated Red, Yellow & green, & water dropping down it, in some Places it tumbled down & broke into small thin Stones like Slate but not hard   amongst the small Stones were pieces of petroleum like pieces of Yellow wax but more triable,[189]   the English Chief tells me its such Rock as this that are about the Country where the Chipperweany get Copper behind the Slaves Lake   at 10 oClk A.M. we have an aft wind & the Men embark   at 12 oClk we perceiv'd a lodge close by the waterside the

[186] "Brant" is not in *Voyages.*

[187] "Boy" is not in *Voyages.*

[188] This depiction of ravenous appetites is quite true. Our group ate more at one meal, while on the river, than we normally ate in a day under normal circumstances. It was not exceptional to eat three or four pounds of fish plus other food at a meal.

[189] "Friable," in *Voyages.* This is the first mention that Mackenzie makes of petroleum. It would be in the area just downriver from present-day Little Chicago. The exact spot would be hard to pinpoint. There are many steep banks and many little rivers falling into the main river in this area.

Natives running about in great confusion & making for the woods, 3 men waited our arrival, they kept at a distance from us their Bows & Arrows in their Hands of which they wanted to shew us the use by snapping the strings, at the same time Making Signs to us not to approach them, the English Chief spoke to them, they understood him a little, I shew'd them some Beads they were afraid to come near to take them, I went up to them and gave them to them, when they first perceiv'd our sails they took us for Eskmeaux who they say have Sails to their larger Canoes, they ask'd us if we had fur from them, & if we had kill'd any of them, likewise if we had seen any of *Diguthe Denue* they thought we had kill'd some of them as they saw us have of their Cloaths Bows &c[190] they appeared to be of the same Tribe tho' they denied it; I suppose through fear, from those questions its evident they had not heard of our being in the Country. they wou'd not own to us that they had any women, tho' we had seen them run into the Wood, they said they left them with more of their Relatives far from the River killing Rein Deer, It was not a long time that they were here their lodge was not finished & they had no fish a drying, they informed us that we should meet with People close by & that there were a great Many at the Rapids,[191] they had a Horn wedge or Chizel with which they split their Canoe wood, this I purchased gave them a Knife & a few more Beads. One of my Indians having broke his Paddle wanted to take one from these people, when he took it up one of them ran immediately to him & took hold of the Paddle & was resolved not to part with it, I was obliged to interfere to prevent his getting a beating & loosing his Paddle & he appear'd very thankful for the Service I had done him. We lost an hour & a half here. The English Chief (& women) were all this time in the wood, they had found their Property but not their Women. they

190 The previous lines appear thus in *Voyages*: "When they first perceived our sail, they took us for the Esquimaux Indians, who employ a sail in their Canoes. They were suspicious of our designs, and questioned us with a view to obtain some knowledge of them. On seeing us in possession of some of the clothes, bows, &c. which must have belonged to some of the Deguthee Denees, or Quarrellers, they imagined, that we had killed some of them, and were bearing away the fruits of our victory."

191 From "They informed" to "Rapids" is omitted in *Voyages*.

took several small things which I did not know of till I had embark'd & left them, or I wou'd have paid for them. The English
Chief is quite enraged against them for running away so, he says
his heart is ill made agt. those Bad Slaves that it is hard to have
come so far & not see the Natives & get nothg from them, that they
hide all their goods & Young Women. We camp'd at 7 oClock[192]
sail'd & paddled since 10 this Morning   soon after we camp'd an
Indian whom we had seen before came to us   his family was at a
little distance up the River   at 9 oClock he left us   fine clear
Weather

SATURDAY 25TH.—we embark'd this Morning[193] past 3   at 7
A.M. passed the Indians lodge   there appears to have been more
than one Family, we suppose that he who came to us last Night
must have given the others a bad opinion of us which made them
run away, their Fire was still alive & they left a good many Fish
scatter'd about their lodge. The weather very sultry the Currt. not
so strong, paddle the most part of the Day   the inland Country
mountainous   the Banks of the River low & well cover'd with
wood among which is the Aspen Tree tho' small & the first I saw
coming up. we saw a Pigeon & a great many Hares. Passed many
Indian Campments which we did not see when we passed down.
aft. 7 oClk the sky to the westward became of a steel Blue colr.
with lightening & thunder   in consequence we landed at ½ past
7 P.M. to prepare ourselves agt. the coming Storm, by the time our
Canoes were unloaded & secured[194] & that we were busy erecting
our Tents it came on with such violence that we expected it would
carry every thing before it. Broke the Ridge Pole of my Tent in the
Middle where it was sound & 9½ Ins in Circumference   we were
obliged to throw ourselves flat upon the ground to escape being
hurt by Stones that were hurled about by the Air like Sand. The

[192] One can only guess as to his campsite this night. This will usually be the case
going up the river. Only when he camped in the same locality coming upriver as he
did going downriver will we know reasonably accurately the location.

[193] *Voyages* inserts "at a quarter." This once again suggests either that a copyist
could have left these words out when copying from the original or that the editor of
Voyages thought more information should be supplied.

[194] "Our Canoes were unloaded & secured" is left out in *Voyages*.

violence of the Storm subsided in a short Time but the Sky continued to be over cast & appearance of Rain

SUNDAY 26TH.—Rain'd hard since early of last Night till this Morning   we embark'd at 4 oClk A.M.   at 8 we landed, at 3 lodges of Indians, they were all asleep, they were much disturbed & frighten'd by our wakeing them tho' the most of them had seen us before, their lodges were hanging as thick with fish as they cou'd hold, we sent some of their Young Men to visit their Nets, they brought us plenty, large white Fish & a round green Fish & a few small white Fish all very good for which I gave them some Beads & made them presents of some more with several other Articles, they were very fond of Iron work of any kind, my Men bot. several Articles for small Pieces of White Iron[195] (Cannister)   there are 5 or 6 Men here that we did not see before among which is a Dog Rib Indian who left his lands on acct. of some Quarrels—The English Chief understood this Man as well as one of his own Nation   he informed us that he understood from the People with whom he now lives (Hare Indians) that there is another large River[196] on the other Side of the Mountains to the S.W. which falls into the *Belhowlay Toe* in comparison to which this is but a small River that the Natives are Big and very wicked, kill Common Men with their Eyes, that they make Canoes larger than Ours that those at the Entry kill a kind of a large Beaver the Skin of which is almost Red, that there has been by Canoes say Ships[197] there often, he knows of no Communication by water to the above River, those of the Natives who saw it went over the Mountains on Foot—he says that there are a few Beaver on this Land which I told him to work & advise the others to do the same & likewise the Martins, Foxes, Beaver,[198] Elic &c wch they might carry to barter for Iron with

195 "Tin," in *Voyages*.

196 Possibly, the Yukon River. In fact, the Yukon is the only river which lies over the mountains to the southwest that is of comparable size to the Mackenzie River. The Indians he met had a tendency to exaggerate sometimes; thus, these asserted that the Yukon was larger than the Mackenzie.

197 These might be Russian traders.

198 After "foxes," "beaver-eaters or wolvereen, &c" are listed in *Voyages*, but not "Elic."

his own Nation, who are now supplied with Goods by French People[199] near their Land. He was very inquisitive to know if we intend to come back this way again, we told him we did not know[200] he told us that it is but few of the Natives who are to be seen along the River that their Young People were killing Rein Deer close by the [201] Eskmeaux Lake where the latter have lately killed one of their Tribe, they say they are very treacherous, that they frequently promise to be Friends which they do not keep longer than they think convenient,[202] they intend to be revenged of them for their last act of Treachery without they pay for the Body of the Person murdered, they say the Eskmeaux Lakes not far off. My Indians wanted to get a young girl that was here, I enquired if they were willing to part with her, but I found that they would not by fair Means, upon no Consideration, had I not prevented my Indians were going to take her by Force, I am obliged to be very watchful over them, for they are always ready to take things from the Natives without giving them anything in return. About 12 oClock we passed a Middling large River from the Eastward, one of the Natives who followed us told us it was called the *Winter Road River*,[203] we did not find the stream strong to day along shore there being many Eddy Currents, we sailed part of the Day, camped at ½ past 7 o'Clock

MONDAY 27TH.—Fine weather, embarked at 20 minutes past 2[204] of the Clock A.M. at 7 landed at 3 Families of Natives close by the Rapid,[205] the Indian that followed us yesterday arrived here some

---

[199] "By us" instead of "by French People," in *Voyages.*

[200] "We told him we did not know" is omitted in *Voyages.*

[201] The handwriting changes.

[202] From "that they frequently" to "convenient" is left out in *Voyages.*

[203] On his journey of the next day, July 27, he arrived near the "Rapid" at "7 A.M." This river could be the present-day Hare Indian River, near which Fort Good Hope is situated. However, he never mentions the Ramparts on his return journey. This is most strange, for he should have gone up them this very afternoon. If the "Rapid" of the next day is the Ramparts, this *Winter Road River* must be any one of a number of other small rivers some thirty or forty miles below present-day Fort Good Hope.

[204] "Half past two," in *Voyages.*

[205] This could refer very easily to the Ramparts because of the Indians mentioned a few lines below, who were to bring in "their Property at a lake close by." Mac-

time before us, we found but few People, we supposed that they hid themselves upon the News of our approach, we remained here about 2 hours, some of the people we had seen before who told us then they had left their Property at a lake close by and had promised to go for them; but they were now no nearer than what they were at that time, they had plenty of Fish, some of which was tied up in Birch Bark—during our stay with them I endeavoured to get some further Intelligence respecting the River I heard of yesterday, they declared to us they knew nothing of it but from hear say, that none of them were [went?] further than the Mountains on the other side of this River, that they were told it was a much larger River than this, that it ran towards the Midday sun, and that there were People a little further up the River who inhabit the opposite Mountain and had lately come down from them to fish, and who knew the other River very well. [206] I promised some Beads to one of them if he would describe the Country round upon the land, this he immediately undertook & perform'd without paying any regard to Courses, he drew a very long pr. of land between the River running into the great lake, at the Extremity of which he said there was a *Belahoulay Cown* white mens Fort,[207] that he did not see but was told of it by other Nations, this I take to be *Unalaschka Fort* & of course the River to the west to be Cooks River & this to fall into or join with Noxta Sound not as a River but a Body of dead water.[208] I ask'd this man if he would go with me across the Mountains to the other River, this he would by no means consent to, alledging that he did not know the Road & that I wou'd get some of the People close by to accompany me as they knew the Road

---

kenzie had met them near what is now Fort Good Hope on his way downstream. It could also refer to the Sans Sault Rapids but it is not likely because of what follows several pages hence.

206 The handwriting changes.

207 "Belhoullay Couin, or White Man's Fort," in *Voyages*. This constant talk of a great river to the west must refer to the Yukon River, and the fort would likely be Russian.

208 From "Cook's River," *Voyages* reads, "and that the body of water or sea into which this river discharges itself at Whale Island, communicates with Norton Sound." No mention is made of "a Body of dead water."

very well, but I believed this more as an excuse than as a truth.
I gave him what I promised him & left them, their is a man of them
who has several Ulcers on his Back, they did not seem to take the
least Care of them, only that a woman was close by him with a
Bunch of Branches[209] in her hand keeping off the Flies. We landed
at the other lodges at 10 oClk A.M. I ordered my men to unload
as I intended to pass the rest of the Day here, in order to get more
familiar with the Natives, that they might answer with less re-
serve any Questions put to them. My young Indians having arrived
here before me, they had some Misunderstanding with the Natives,
who upon their arrival & before the[y] debark'd took hold of their
Canoe pull'd it on the Shore, the wet. of the People in it Broke it,
this they took as an assult & was going to avenge it as such, had I
not come up to prevent it. I find the variation of the Compass to be
abt. 29 degrees Easterly   at 4 P.M. I ordered my Interpreter to
harangue them in Council, after a long discourse cou'd learn very
little satisfactory Intelligence, what they said regarding the River
to the Westward agreed with what we had already heard but what
they say of the Inhabitants is still more absurd; that they are very
big, have wings but don't fly, that they live upon large Birds which
they kill with ease, tho' those Birds would kill common men if
they would approach them, that the People at the Entry of the
River kill men with their Eyes & live upon large Beaver one of
which they devour at a meal that large Canoes come to this Place
&c. &c.   all this they heard from other People   they were never
further than the first Mountains to kill the small white Buffaloe
that the Sources of the River which comes into this River & those
that fall into the others are separated by the Mountains, & that
they are all very Small that the People on the other Side of the
Mountains kill them where they meet. Its very certain that those
People know more about the Country than they chuse to tell me at
least than what comes to my Ears. I am obliged to depend upon my
Interpreter for all News, his being now & long since tired of the
Voyage may occasion him to conceal from me part of what the

[209] "Feathers" instead of "branches," in *Voyages*.

Natives tell him for fear he should be obliged to undergo more fatigues[210]—tho' he has always declared to me that he would not abandon me wherever I went, as soon as we left them they began their fav'rite & only Amusement (except Jumpg.) Dancg. in which Young & Old, Male & Female join'd & continued as they could hold out—They try to imitate the Rein Deer Bear & Wold [?] in their Pranks or howling. When this Pastime was over I made the English Chief again begin to discourse with them on the former Topic, but with no better success than before. [211] I appeared to be quite angry with and made him tell them, that I thought they did not tell me the Truth, and that if they did not tell me every thing they know, that one of them must come along with me tomorrow to show me the road to the other River, for which I would give him Iron work and Beads for pains, upon which they all to a man became sick and answered in a very sickly Tone, that they knew no more than what they had already told that they would die if I took any of them, that they knew nothing of the Road   they began to dissuade my Interpreter from going by telling him that they loved him like themselves, and if he would go he should be killed &c, this and the solicitation of his women seemed to have the desired effect upon him tho' he hid it from me. I can expect no other account of the country or the other great River, till I get to the River of the Bear lake, where I expect to find some of the Natives who promised to wait us there, and who had mentioned this River to me when we passed them, which I paid no attention to them. as I thot. it was a misunderstanding of my Interpreters. or what they might have invented along with their other lies to prevent my proceeding down the River, we are well supplied with Fish, dry and fresh, by these People. they likewise gathered as many *husk* or whurtle Berries for us as we chose, all which accepted Beads, Awls, Knives and pieces of white Iron,[212] I traded a few Beaver Skins from them, they say that they are not very numerous on their lands, that there are likewise

210 The next lines are omitted in *Voyages*. It continues immediately with "No sooner was the conference concluded, than they began to dance."
211 The handwriting changes.
212 "Tin," in *Voyages*.

a few Moor[213] Deer and Buffaloes, They begged of us not to hurt some of their young Men who were killing geese upon Islands above here—I made all the men presents of a few trifling articles, at Sun Set I was obliged to shoot one of their Dogs, all day we could not keep them away from our Baggage, I had told them before to keep them away but they paid no attention to me, when they heard the report of the Pistol and saw the dog dead, they got terribly frighted   the women took their children on their Backs to run into the woods,[214] I made the English Chief tell them that the Dog was kill'd because he stole our provisions, and to tie all the rest of their Dogs if they did not chose they should be used in the same manner,[215] but that they need not be afraid themselves that we should do them no hurt. The woman to whom the Dog belonged to was crying bitterly, and said she had lost 5 children last Winter for whom she was not so sorry as for the Dog. I gave her a few Beads and an awl, and all was over, it does not require much reason to make the Men or women cry or feign Sickness, when we arrived this day the latter were all in Tears, and we since learn'd that it was for fear that we should take any of them away with us, indeed they are not very tempting objects, for they are as ugly and disagreeable Beings as can be, notwithstanding wch[216] one of our married men and one of the Hunters got the better of their feelings, and prevailed with two of the above objects to accept of a share of their Bed for the night, the reward a small knife, but in place of a Farrian each they had three, the young men having invited their Companions to partake of their favours, however. the recompense was augmented in proportion[217]—One of the upper part of the Beach here grow plenty of liquorice, its now in Blossom, I pulled up some of the Roots and eat them. I asked the Natives if they made use of it, told me not, some of the Roots very large and long.

213 "Moose-deer," in *Voyages*.
214 "Ran into the woods," in *Voyages*.
215 From "and to tie" to "same manner" is omitted in *Voyages*.
216 The "wch" is an insert in the Journal, in the same handwriting however.
217 From "and prevailed" to "Proportion" is not in *Voyages*.

TUESDAY 28TH.—At 4 this morning, I ordered my men to load our Canoe, during which time I went with the English Chief up to the lodges, and found that the most of them had decamp'd in the Night, those that were remaining were all so sick that they could not rise for fear that I should take any of them along with me, they all said that they would kill Beaver and Martins plenty because the French People were fond of their skins   They were quite happy when they saw we did not take any of them with us. after we got into our Canoe they came out of their lodges and told us to visit their Nets that were a little way up the River and take all the Fish in them, we took as many as we wanted, we debarked shortly after at 2 Lodges full of Fish, there were no people there, we supposed they were amongst those we had just[218] left, my Indians rumaged both lodges and found several small articles which they took a liking to, I gave them Beads and Awls to put in their places, but they did not understand why this should be left as the owners were not present, they wanted to keep both, I took up a Net out of the water and left a Big Knife in place of it. It is not above 4 fms long and it is 32 Meshes deep. those nets are much more convenient to set in the Eddy country than our long ones. This is the place that the Indians call the Rapid, we came up it all the way with the Paddle, so that the Currt. is not near so strong here as in the many other parts of the River, and it is well it is so, for it would be very difficult coming up with line, there being no Beach in many places and the Rocks high and perpendicular, rather hanging over the water;[219] hundreds of Swallows nests in those Rocks   very sultry weather, at 11 oClk obliged to land to gum our Canoe, this is the first time we landed for this purpose since we left Athabasca,[220] in less than an hour we got ready for marching. At 1 oClk we put on shore at a fire which we suppos'd had been kindled by the young men that were hunting geese. Our Hunters found their

[218] Again "just" is inserted in the Journal above the line.
[219] This area is more likely the Rampart area, which means that Mackenzie has spent the last day between present-day Fort Good Hope and the entrance to the Ramparts.
[220] From "this is the first" to "we left Athabasca," is left out in *Voyages*.

Canoe and Fowl hid in the Wood, they shortly after discovered their Owners and brought them to the waterside, out of upwards of 200 geese we picked 36 of which were eatable, the rest were quite green and stunk abominably, it was some time since they had killed them, and not gutted them   we could not imagine that any people would eat Rotteness were we not persuaded they do. I paid for those we had taken and departed   at 7 P.M. the weather became cloudy and overcast, at 8 we camp'd, at 9 it began to lighten and thunder very severely, soon after came on a perfect Hurricane and heavy rain, blew down our Tents, and was like to carry away our Canoe, which we fasten'd down to Trees with a Cod line, it lasted 2 Hours and soaked us completely. We are obliged to throw away part of the Fowls, we embarked today.[221]

WEDNESDAY 29TH.—The weather cloudy, yesterday the Heat was insupportable, and today we can't put clothes enough on to keep us warm, embarked at a quarter past 4   aft wand [wind?] which drove us on at a great rate   the Current is very strong, about 10 oClk we came to the other rapid, which we came up with the line, on the west side[222]   found it much stronger than when we went down, the water has fallen at least 6 feet[223] and has uncovered many Beaches in the River, which we had not seen. One of my young Hunters was liked to get drown'd crossing a River that falls in here from the Westward,[224] its the most considerable one except the River of the Mountains that comes from this Direction. A strong North wind all day and cold, camp'd at a quarter past 8, we killed a goose and catched some young ones

SATURDAY[225] 30TH.—Embark'd at 4 oClock this morning, rained hard last night, cloudy weather, but not so cold as Yesterday wind N.W. sailed part of the Day, camp'd at half past [blank

221 The last sentence is omitted in *Voyages*.

222 Most likely the Sans Sault Rapids. The lower the water level in the river the stronger the rapids are. The west side is far easier to navigate up or down than the east side.

223 "Five feet," in *Voyages*.

224 Today Mountain River.

225 *Voyages* has, correctly, "Thursday 30."

space[226]] P.M. we killed 5 old geese and 30 young ones. The Indians killed 6 old and 10 young ones. The English Chief had a dispute with one of his young men, he discovered that he was too intimate with his young wife, and that she was to run away with him when they would get to their own Country.[227] This is all I could learn of their Discourse This 2 or 3 Days past we have eat a good deal of the liquorice Root, plenty of which is along the River we find it a good astringent.

FRIDAY 31ST.—Rained all night and till 9 this morning when we embark'd, the wind and weather as yesterday about 3 P.M. clear'd up the wind died away and became warm. At 5 Easterly wind and cold, plenty of whurtle Berries, Rasberries &c.[228] along the Bank, we are much impeded in our march by Banks of Sand and small Stones, which rinders the water shallow at a distance from the shore. In other Places the Bank of the River is high of black Earth and Sand continually tumbling, in some part shews a face of solid Ice, to within a foot of the Surface, we camp'd at a quarter before 8 we killed 5 geese, Our Indians 2, my foreman had some words with the latter for mimicking his way of Paddling.[229] Tonight we begin upon our corn, we ate only 3 Days upon our Provisions since we began to mount the Curt. it was my Intention to have gone up the River on the South Side from the last rapid to see if there are any Rivers of consequence coming in from the westward, but the No. of Sand Banks & the Current being too strong obliges me to Traverse to the old Side where the Eddy Currents are very frequent wherein we can set out Nets, & make much more headway—

AUGUST 1789

SATURDAY 1ST. AUGT.—Embark'd at 3 this morning weather clear & cold wind S.E. at 3 P.M. we travers'd & landed to take the

---

[226] This is blank in the Journal. *Voyages* has "about seven," perhaps merely because of a lack of any other number.

[227] The part about their plans to run away is left out in *Voyages*.

[228] "And a berry called *Poire*, which grows in the greatest abundance" instead of "&c." in *Voyages*.

[229] "My foreman had some words with the latter for mimicking his way of Paddling" is left out of *Voyages*.

line, here is a Campment of the Natives apparently as if they had
left it yesterday, at 5 oClk we found a Man, 2 women, & 2 children
Camp'd close by the water side we had not seen them before
they have but few fish,[1] we enquired if there were any of their
Friends close by, say not, except a lodge on the otherside & a man
from this a hunting I find my Interpreter rather averse to ask
such questions as I desire him, I believe he is afraid that I might get
some intelligence which wou'd prevent his seeing Athabasca this
Season, if he would act as he ought, we left him with the Indian,
we camp'd at ½ past 7 at our Campmt. of the 5TH ulto.[2] The Indian
came along with the English Chief to our Fire, he says that it is
not many Nights since the Indian who went down part of the River
with us had passed here; that we wou'd meet with 3 lodges of his
People above the River of the Bear Lake, that he knows nothg. of
the River to the Westward, only that he heard his Friends say there
was such a Thing Tonight is the first Time it has been dark
enough to see a Star since we left Athabaska.

SUNDAY 2D.—we got under weigh with the line at 3 this Morng.
I walk'd along with the Indians as they went faster than my Men
particularly today as they wanted to arrive at the Natives before
us, I observ'd several small Springs of Mineral Water running from
under the Mountains, & along the Beach many lumps[3] of Iron ore
when we came to the River of the Bear Lake I made one of the
young Indians remain for my Canoe & took his Place in the Small
Canoe, this River is abt. 250 Yds. wide here,[4] the water quite clear
of a Sea Colour, where I landed on the opposite Shore found that
the Natives had been lately here from the print of their feet in
the Sand, we contd. walking on till 6 oClk A.M.[5] when we saw several
Smokes along the Shore, we made ourselves sure those were the

---

[1] The handwriting changes.

[2] "The fifth of last month," in *Voyages*. Mackenzie is now only a few miles below
the mouth of Great Bear River.

[3] "Several lumps," in *Voyages*.

[4] Going downriver Mackenzie thought this river was "100 yd" wide (see footnote
56 of "July 1789"). Actually the river is about one-quarter mile wide.

[5] "Five in the afternoon," in *Voyages*, which is obviously a mistake because of
what follows.

Natives we were to meet with, therefore—hasten'd our Pace as we approach'd we found a sulpherous Smell & upon our coming to the first Sound that the whole Bank was on Fire for a considerable Distance. that it is a Coal Mine the Fire had communicated to it from an old Indian Campmt.[6] The Beach is cover'd with Coals The English Chief gather'd some of the softest he cou'd find to dye Blk, he says it is with this the Natives colour their Quilles Blk. here we waited for the big Canoe which arrived an hour afterwards at half past 10 oClk we saw several Indians Marks which[7] pointed to the woods opposite to wh is an old Beaten Road & it appear'd People had lately passed in it. the Beach is cover'd with Tracks a little further were the Poles of 5 lodges standg. here we landed & unloaded our Canoe. I dispatch'd a Frenchman to see if he could find any Natives within a Days March of us. I wanted the English Chief to go; but he wou'd not saying that he was too much fatigued & the Young Men wou'd Answer the same Purpose, as we had already seen those People that they wou'd not hesitate comg. to see us. This is the first time he refus'd me & I believe its from Jealousy, tho' I have taken every precaution it shou'd not be of the Frenchmen.[8] No appearance of Snow on the opposite Mountains, tho' they were almost covered with it when we passed before. Set 2 Nets. At 11 oClk at Nt. the Frenchmen & Indian return'd they had been to the first Campmt. where there were 4 Fires, its not long since the Natives had left it. they were obliged to make the Tour of several small lakes wh the Natives cross with their small Canoes. the Encampt. was on the Border of a Lake which was too large to go round & prevented their going any further. they saw several Beavers & Beaver lodges in those small lakes, they kill'd one, its Fur, begin to get long, which is a sure sign of the approach of the Fall. They likewise saw the track of Moor[9] & Rein Deer plenty but old. This being the Time that the Rein Deer leaves the

---

[6] This area is still burning today because of the coal deposits.

[7] *Voyages* inserts "consisted of pieces of bark fixed on poles, and pointing to the woods."

[8] "Canadians," in *Voyages*.

[9] "Moose," in *Voyages*.

Plains to come to the wood as the Musquittoes time is almost over. makes me apprehensive that we will not find a single Indian on the River Side as they will be in or abt. the Mountains setting Snares to catch Careboeuff.[10]

MONDAY 3D.—we got underway at 4 this Morng. strong westerly wind. Cloudy cold weather   at 12 oClk the weather clear'd up & became fine. the Currt. very strong the water has fallen much since we passed, discover'd many Banks which were not visible   kill'd 4 geese of a larger kind than usual. saw sevl. Indian Campments along the River. Landed for the Night 8 oClk P.M.

TUESDAY 4TH.—at 4 oClk this morng. we got underway fine calm. There fell a very heavy Dew last Night & was cold. unloaded our Canoe at 9 oClk A.M. to gum lost abt. an Hours time. The weather warming   saw many tracks of Rein Deer along the Water Side. Camp'd at half past 6[11] to set our Nets   the Currt. very strong all Day & difficult walking along the Beach.

TUESDAY [WEDNESDAY] 5TH.—rose our Nets without a single Fish   the water is so low that there is not Room in the Eddy Currt. to set nets. Currt. strong as yesterday bad walking. the Beach is large Stones. it is so cold today that our marchg. don't keep us warm with all our clothes on—at Noon yesterday we found our Shirt too heavy   past several Points to Day, had we been loaded we should have been obliged to unload to have come up them. Camp'd at 6 oClk very much fatigued. The Indians kill'd 4 geese[12] the mens two   Women are continually employ'd making shoes[13] as a pair does not last us above one Day, of course [the women?] don't debark out of the Canoe.

THURSDAY 6TH.—Rain'd last night & this Morning which prevented our getting on our way till ½ past 6 A.M.   a strong aft wind which with the help of our Paddles drove us on at a good rate. We landed at 6 oClk & camp'd to wait our Indians who we have not

---

[10] *Voyages* merely states "to take them," referring to the reindeer and making no mention of "Careboeuff."

[11] "Half past five," in *Voyages*.

[12] "2 geese," in *Voyages*.

[13] "Of Moose-skin" is added in *Voyages*.

seen since morning at ½ past 7   they arriv'd in a very ill humour, we have not seen the least appearance of Indian Campments since the Day before yesterday.

TUESDAY[14] 7TH.—commenced our Day at ½ past 3 this Morng.   shortly after we saw two Rein Deer on the Beach a head, we stopp'd & our Indians went to approach them, but they were too ambitious who shou'd first get near them, that they rais'd the animals, of course lost them. at the same time we saw an Animal traversing, we immediately made for it & killed it, it proved to be a Rein Deer Female & from the No. of Cuts she had in the hind Legs we judged she had been pursued by Wolves & that they had destroyed her young ones. her udder was full of Milk, one of the young Indians cut it up & emptied the Milk among some boiled Corn & ate it declaring it was (*Wicazen*) delicious   at 5 P.M. we saw an Animal running along the Beach which some said was a Dog & others said was a Grey Fox, soon after I put a shore for the Night at the Entrance of a small River, as I thot. there might be some Natives not far off. I ordered my Hunters to arrange their Fuzees & gave them ammunition to go a hunting Tomorrow & at the same Time to look out for Natives in the Neighboring Mountains. I found a small Canoe in the edge of the Wood, had a Paddle & Bow in it, it had been mended this Spring, the Bark was much neater sewed than any I had yet seen—we saw many old Campmts. in the Course of the Day. the Current very strong & point equal to rapids.

SATURDAY 8TH.—rain'd exceeding hard all last Night & this Day till past Noon when it clear'd up a little. Strong westerly wind & cold. at 3 oClk the Indians went a Hunting   at 8 they return'd without having kill'd any thing, they saw plenty Rein Deer Tracks. the[y][15] fell upon an old Beaten Path wh one of them follow'd for some time, he said it did not appear that any of the Natives had passed it for some time past. It began again to rain & continued till the Morning.

14 "Friday," in *Voyages*.
15 "They," in *Voyages*.

SUNDAY 9TH.—we embark'd at half past 3 A.M. the weather Cloudy & cold   at 10 it clear'd up weather calm & moderate   saw a small Canoe in the Edge of the Woods, one of the Indians kill'd a Dog very poor, saw a No. of Places where the Natives had made Fire, by which it appear'd that they do not remain a long time along the River, that they cross from one Side to the other, we saw some Roads which were cut upon each Side opposite to one another, we perceiv'd that the Water rose considerable since last Night. found the Currt. strong all Day   we camp'd at 7 oClk.

MONDAY 10TH.—embark'd at 3 this Morning fine clear weather at light wind[16] from the S.E.   the Indians went ahead a huntg. loaded[17] at 10 oClk opposite to the Mountains we had passed the 2d. tillts[18] to try to ascertain the variation of the Compass at this Place which I cou'd do but imperfectly as I cannot depend on my watch. I find it about 27 degrees Easterly   one of my Hunters join'd us here   he had walked all Day not kill'd any thing, as this opposite-Mountains are the last considerable ones on the S.W. Side of the River I ordd. my Men to Traverse the River that I wanted to ascent one of the Mountains,[19] it was near 4 before we landed, I immediately set off accompanied by the young Indian my men being more fatigued than curious: & we soon began to experience that we wou'd pay for ours, the Wood which is chiefly Epinettes[20] was so thick that it was with much ado we cou'd make our Way thro' it, after we had walked upwards of an Hours time, the Wood became thinner of the white Birch & Aspen[21] Kind, the former was the largest & tallest that I had ever seen, when we had travers'd this the ground began to rise & [was] cover'd with small Pines,

---

[16] "A light wind," in *Voyages*.

[17] "Landed," in *Voyages*.

[18] "Second of the last month," in *Voyages*. This would not be far from present-day Camsell Bend. He is making good time for coming up against the current. In twenty days Mackenzie has traveled over six hundred miles upstream in spite of weather and frequent stops—an average of thirty miles a day.

[19] The mountains here look very close to the river, but Mackenzie's experience proves that they are not.

[20] "Spruce firs," in *Voyages*.

[21] "Poplar," in *Voyages*.

here we got the first View of the Mountains since we left the Canoe upwards of 3 Hours walking; and they appear'd as far from us as when we had seen them from the River;[22] My Companion wanted absolutely to return, his Shoes & leggins were all torn to Pieces, besides he said that we wou'd not be able to return thro' such bad Road in the Night, however I persisted in proceeding & that we wou'd pass the Night in the Mountains & return in the Morning as we approach'd them the grd became quite Marshy & we waded in Water & grass up to the Middle[23] till we came within a Mile of the Foot of the Mountains, where I fell in up to the Arm Pits & with some difficulty extricated myself   I found it impossible to proceed in a St. Line & the Marsh extended as far as I could see, so that I did not attempt to make the Circuit, so therefore thought it most prudent to make the best of my Way back to my Canoe (tho it was Night when I arrived after 12 oClk very much fatigued.

TUESDAY 11TH.—we observed several Tracks along the Beach & a Campt. in the Edge of the Wood which appeared to be 5 or 6 Days old, we would have continued our Rout along this Side the River were it not that we have not seen our Hunters since Yesterday Morng.   we embark'd before 3 A.M. & travers'd   at 5 we see two of them comg. down the River in search of us, as they were surprised what detained us. They kill'd no large Animals, only one Beaver & a few Hares, & they said that the Wood was so thick near the River that it was impossible to hunt, they had seen several of the Natives Campments not far from the River, & they were of Opinion that they were here when we passed downwards & their having discovered us is the Reason that we meet with none of them now. I asked the English Chief to return with me to the other Side to endeavor to find those whose Track & Campments we had seen, which he was not willing to do,[24] he wanted to send the Young Men

22 It is very difficult to say just how far these mountains are from the river, but I would guess that the closest would be approximately fifteen to twenty miles, perhaps more, to its summit. With the record of Mackenzie's experience before us we did not get curious.

23 "Up to the knees," in *Voyages.*

24 In *Voyages* the English Chief is not so blunt: "but he was backward in complying with my desire."

but I cou'd not trust them & am very doubtful me [of?] himself they are still afraid that I may meet with the Natives who might give me Accts. of the other River & that I should go over land to it, & bring them along with me. I was told today by one of my men that the English Chief his wives & Brother[25] were to leave me, this Side of the Slave Lake to go to the Land of the Beaver Indians, & again the Middle of the Winter he wou'd be back to the Slave Lake where he was to meet some of his Relations who went to War last Spring to whom he had given Rendayvous. [26] this he learn'd from one of the Young Men,[27] we traversed and continued tracking the Indians till past 12 o'Clock when we lost their Tracks, we supposed they must have crossed to the East side, we saw several Dogs on each side of the River, The young Indians killed a Wolf, which is fat, the Men eat it and declared it to be very good   killed 15 young geese which are big and begin to fly   It was 8 OClock when we camp'd, lost upwards of 4 hours to day traversing, fine weather all Day

WEDNESDAY 12TH.—all embarked at 3 this Morning sent the young Indians across, that we might not miss any of the Natives should there be any along the River   We saw many places where they had made Fire along the Beach, none of them old and fire running in the Wood in many places. At 4 oClock we came to a Campment which the People had left this Morning   we found there Tracks in several Places in the Woods as I thought they could not be far off. I asked the English Chief to go and try, if he could find them which he seemed to loath to do, I told him I intended to go with him, and he could not be oft, we started and went several Miles into the wood but we could not find any thing of them, the fire had ran all over the country, burnt abt. 3 ins. of blk lt. soil which covered a cold body of Clay and which was so hard that the Feet left no Track, at 10 o'Clock we returned from our fruitless Excursion. The young men kill'd 7 Geese, had several

---

[25] "Companions" instead of "brother," in *Voyages*.
[26] The handwriting changes.
[27] "This he learn'd from one of the young Men" is not in *Voyages*.

showers of Rain with gusts of wind and Thunder. The men set nets during my absense.

THURSDAY 13TH.—Rose our Nets without a single Fish and embark'd at half past 3 A.M. Fine weather, pass a No. of Places where the Natives had made Fires, and many Tracks along the Beach. At 7 o'Clk we came opposite the Island where we had hid our Pemmican, 2 of the young Indians went for it, and found it as we had left it, and is very acceptable to us, as it will enable us to get out of the River without losing much time to hunt, shortly after we perceived a smook on the S.W. Shore, 3 Leagues distant, it did not appear to be a running fire. The Indians were a little way ahead of us, and paid no attention to this smook, they saw a flock of geese ahead which they fired several shot on, and we immediately perceived that the Smook disappeared, and soon after saw the Natives run along the Shore and soon embarking in their small Canoes, tho' we were almost opposite to them, we could not think of traversing witht. going further upon account of the Strength of the Current, I ordered the Indians to make all the haste they could to go and speak with, and make them wait our arrival, as soon as our small Canoe struck off we could see the Natives that were in their Canoes landing, drawing their Canoes on the Beach and making for the Wood, It was past 10 A.M. before we landed at where they left their Canoes which were 4 in Number, They were in such Terror that they left a Number of their Things on the Beach, they did not wait the arrival of our Indians, the latter I found busy running along[28] among the Things and looking for more in the wood, I was very vex'd at them, that instead of looking for the Natives, they were separating their Property for which I severely rebuked the English Chief, I ordered him his young men and my own men to go and look out for the Indians, I went also, but they were too much frightened and had too much the start of [for?] us to ever take them, we saw several Dogs in the woods some of which followed us to the water side. The English Chief was very much

[28] "Along" is very indistinct—almost blotted out as if by a wet sponge—in the Journal.

displeased that I had reproach'd him, and told me so, I waited such an opportunity to tell him his Behaviour to me for some time past, told him that I had more reason to be angry than he, that I had come a great way at a great Expense to no Purpose, and that I thot. he hid from me part of what the Natives told him respecting the Country &c. for fear that he should have to follow me, and that his Reason for not killing[29] was his Jealousy, which likewise kept him from looking for the Natives, as he ought, and that we never had given him any reason for such Suspicion.

He got into a most violent passion, and said, we spoke ill, that he was not jealous, that he had not concealed any thing from us, and that till now there were no Animals, and that he would not accompany us any further tho' he was without ammunition, he cou'd live the same as the Slaves, and that he would remain among them &c. &c. as soon as he was done his Harrangue he began to cry bitterly, and his relations help'd him, they said they cried dead Friend,[30] I did not interrupt them in their grief for two Hours, as I could not well without them, I was obliged to use every method to make the English Chief change his mind, at last he consented with a great Reluctance,[31] and we embark'd I sent the young Men across the River in case we should meet with any more of the Natives they could not escape from us so easily What the Natives left behind were Bows, arrows, Snares for Moor and Rein Deer, and for Hares, Fishing Hooks and lines, Nets, a few Bark Dishes, a few Martin and Beaver, old Beaver Robes, and a small Robe made of *Loopserviers*.[32] Their Canoes are curiously made of the Bark of the Epinette, and can carry two or three People, I ordered my Men to put their Canoes into the Shade gave the most of other things to the Indians (young) the English Chief would not accept of any of them, I left in place of them fastened upon 3 high poles,[33] 2 small pieces of Cloth, small knives, a File, Beads, awls, 2 Fire

[29] "Game" must be understood here. *Voyages* has "killing game, &c."
[30] "For their dead friends," in *Voyages*.
[31] From "Reluctance" to "easily" is omitted in *Voyages*.
[32] "Lynx" in *Voyages*.
[33] *Voyages* does not mention the fastening of anything to "3 high poles."

Steels, a comb, Rings, got a Martin put upon a proper Mould, as they were not properly moulded, and a Beaver Skin stretched upon a Frame, to which I tied a scraper, the Indians are of opinion that the above Articles will be lost as the Natives are so frightened that they will not back here any more, we lost 6 Hours at this place, 3 of the Dogs followed us along the Beach, camp'd at half past 8 close by the Entrance of the River of the Mountains,[34] while the men were unloading I took a walk along the Beach and are Banks which were uncovered since we past down by the water falling were all over white with fine Particles of Salt. I invited the English Chief to sup with me, I gave him a Dram or two and were as good friends as ever. he told me that it was the Custom of the Chipewean Chiefs to go to war after the Crees,[35] and that next Spring he should go for certain, that he would remain and do as he used to do for the French people till that time,[36] gave him a little grog to carry to his Tent to drown his Chagrine, the Indians killed 3 geese today, fair weather.

FRIDAY 14TH.—we embarked at a quarter before 4 A.M. we went about 2 Miles into the River of the Mountains   fire on each side of it in the grod., in traversing I sounded it and found 5–4½ and 3½ fm water which is quite muddy and keeps of [from?] the grand River on the West side down to what we call the last Rapid where it meets together.[37] passed several of the natives Campments.

[34] Mackenzie is once more near present-day Fort Simpson. He had not averaged quite thirty miles a day for the past three days.

[35] *Voyages* states, "it was a custom with the Chepewyan chiefs to go to war after they had shed tears, in order to wipe away the disgrace attached to such a feminine weakness." It is possible that the copyist could have made a mistake and used "the Crees" instead of "they Cried" since there seems to be an eraser mark and a possibility of "y" being erased from "the" and the "s" of "Crees" being made out of a "d" with the top erased. If this is the case, the Journal should read "after they cried" instead of "after the Crees." On the other hand it could mean what it says, for the Crees and Chipewyans were not above fighting each other.

[36] *Voyages* does not mention service to the French but states thus: "at the same time he declared his intention to continue with us as long as I should want him."

[37] *Voyages* adds "It was impossible not to consider it as an extraordinary circumstance, that the current of the former river should not incorporate with that of the latter, but flow, as it were, in distinct streams at so great a distance, and till the contracted state of the channel unites them."

A River on the North side which appeared to be navigable, we camp'd at ½ past 6 P.M. plenty of Berries which the men call *poires*, they are purple bigger than a Pea, very well Tasted, some goose Berries and a few Straw berries.

SATURDAY 15TH.—we embark'd at 3 oClk this morning till 2 P.M. saw many Campments, along the water side, since which time very little Beach. Banks of the River high and no Eddy Current, we camp'd at ½ past 5 P.M. The Indians killed 12 geese,[38] very sultry all Day

SUNDAY 14TH.[39]—Embarked at a quarter before 4 A.M. past our Campment of the 30th[40] June 9 oClk A.M., here the River is wide and flat along shore, the land on the North side low, soil black, mixt with Stone well covered with Aspin, Poplar, white Birch, Epinette &c. the Current is not strong, we go up it nearly as fast as in dead water, at 12 we passed a Campment of 3 Fires, the only one we saw this Day the weather as Yesterday.

MONDAY 17TH.—Embarked at half past 3 A.M., we passed 3 Campments, by the manner their *Shude*[41] were made we think that some of the Red Knives must have come down this length and seen some of the Natives tho it is not customary with them to come this way, I arranged the young Indians late last Night to go ahead to hunt, over took them at 10 oClock, they had killed some, 5 young Swans, the English Chief killed an Eagle, 3 Cranes, a small Beaver, and 2 geese, we camped at our Camp of the 29th[42] June last 7 oClk. P.M.[43] My foreman who lead the March had some words with one

[38] *Voyages* adds "berries were collected in great abundance."

[39] "Sunday 16," in *Voyages*, which would seem to be right.

[40] "13th of June," in *Voyages*. This must be wrong, for their camp of that day was many miles away on Great Slave Lake. Their camp of June 30th was about seventy miles upriver from present-day Fort Simpson where they camped on August 13; thus, they were making about thirty miles a day August 14 and August 15 according to the date used in the Journal.

[41] "Huts," in *Voyages*.

[42] *Voyages* uses this same date, which supports the hypothesis that the "13th of June" of footnote 40 of the previous page must be incorrect. This also suggests that Mackenzie and his men put in a very full day, for they had paddled over fifty miles upstream.

[43] Here *Voyages* concludes the day's events. The next lines are left out completely, with no mention made of the disagreement or loss of the gun.

of my Steersmen for hard marching, that he did not give them time to eat or smook &c. they wanted to land to see who was the best man, but it was not deemed necessary to comply with their request, I interfered and all was over, this is the first and only dispute of the kind that we have had since we commenced our Voyage, One of the young Indians lost a gun belonging to one of the Men, it fell overboard out of his Canoe

TUESDAY 18TH.—at 4 this Morning I equipped all the Indians to go a hunting and sent them ahead, as our Stock of Provision is nearly out, We embarked at half past 6 and we traversed to the North Shore where the land was low and almost out of Sight,[44] it was near 12 when we arrived   I had an observation which gave

$$41.2^{45}$$
$$16$$
$$\overline{}$$
$$41.18$$
$$12.51$$
$$\overline{}$$
$$28.27$$
$$90.$$
$$\overline{}$$
$$61.33$$

we were near 6 Miles[46] to the N. of the Main Channel of the River, there were the Tracks and Beds of a No. of Buffaloes here fresh A River close by which comes from the Horn Mountains,[47] not far off, at 5 oClk P.M. we landed when the Indians had gone ahunting before the Canoe was unloaded the English Chief arrived with the Tongue of a Cow, 4 Men and 2 Indians went for the Meat, It was dark before they came back, the Indians tell me they saw several

44 "Scarcely visible in the horizon," in *Voyages*.
45 *Voyages* gives the observation merely as "61.33 North latitude."
46 "Five miles," in *Voyages*. The "North Shore" is well over six miles from the "Main Channel" at its most northerly point. The area is known today as Mills Lake.
47 Today the Horn River.

Tracks in the Sand on the opposite Island, they killed 5 Geese, we came the value of 8 Hours good Marching today[48]

WEDNESDAY 19TH.—Sent the Indians again ahead, to go a hunting when they choosed, the men gummed their Canoe, having had no time to do it last Night, and we embarked at half past 5 A.M. and at 9 A.M. landed where the Indians went a hunting to wait their return   I found the Variation of the Compass here to be about 20 Degrees Easterly. The Men made themselves Paddles and repaired the Canoes, I observe that the mens Paddles Row very fast in the water of this River, I do not know what this may be owing to its some quality in the water;[49] The Hunters arrived late without meeting with any large Animals, they killed 3 Swans and 3 geese,[50] the women gathered plenty of small Cramberries.[51]

THURSDAY 20TH.—we embarked at 4 oClk A.M., made the Men follow the North side of the River, tho' the Currt. is much stronger, to see the River, which the Indians had mentioned to me when going down as coming from the Land of the Beaver Indians and falling in here about, but there proved to be none here, and [I decided?] that he meant the River which we passed the Day before Yesterday (on the line)[52]   the Current very strong   traversed to a Island opposite, here the Current is still stronger, like a Rapid, found a Paddle and an Awl on the Water side. The former we knew to be the Crees.[53] I suppose it must be the *Mirde Dours*[54] and his Party who went to War last year, and has taken this Route on their return to Athabasca, and probably they must have been the cause of our not seeing many Natives along the River. The weather Raw

---

[48] This last clause is not in *Voyages* but instead "The fine weather continued without interruption." At about three miles or better an hour this would suggest about twenty-five to thirty miles. He probably camped near present-day Fort Providence.

[49] In *Voyages*: "there is some peculiar quality of the water in this river, which corrodes the wood, from the destructive effect it had on the paddles."

[50] "Many geese," in *Voyages*.

[51] "Crowberries" also, in *Voyages*.

[52] "On the line" is omitted in *Voyages*.

[53] "The Knistineaux," in *Voyages*.

[54] "Chief Merde-d'ours," in *Voyages*.

and Cloudy which we find very disagreeable It having been so fine and warm several Days before, we camped at half past 7 P.M. on the North Side where the land is very low and flat to come near the Shore.[55] The Indians killed 5 young Swan and missed a Bear.[56] Appearance of Rain

FRIDAY 21ST.—Weather cold, a very strong easterly wind, frequent showers of Rain which detained us in our Campement all Day. In the afternoon the Indians went on the Track of a Moose Deer, had no luck.

SATURDAY 22D.—The wind veered round to the Westward, still very strong and cold as yesterday, we embarked and in 3 hours time came to the Entrance of *the Slave Lake* under half sail with the Paddle,[57] it would have taken us at least 8 hours to come it, the Indians did not arrive till 4 hours after us. The wind is too strong to attempt going in the Lake, set a Net, and camp'd for the Night, the women gathered plenty of Berries viz. *quieide Pouilles,*[58] Cramberries Crow Berries, and original Berries. The Indians killed 2 Swans 1 geese. The men 2 geese

SUNDAY 23D.—Embarked at 5 A.M. rose our Nets. Caught 5 small Pike, entered the Lake thro' the same Entrance we came out of it, tho' South side of the Lake would be the shortest road, but we are not sure of there being a good Fishery along the Coast, and we are certain of catching plenty the way we came, besides I expect to find Mr. Leroux[59] where I left him, having given him orders to remain there till the Fall,[60] and I can leave what goods I have left with him, If I find it necessary he should winter, we paddled along

---

[55] This would suggest that he camped somewhere near the west end of present-day Beaver Lake.

[56] "The Indians killed five young swans, and a beaver," in *Voyages.*

[57] It has taken Mackenzie thirty-two days to make about 910 miles from Separation Point into Great Slave Lake as compared with a little better than thirteen days which he spent covering the same distance going with the current. If we subtract the time lost by storm and exploration going both directions, he averaged nearly 100 miles a day going downstream and better than 30 miles a day going upstream. This is a phenomenal record and indicates that his men worked very well.

[58] "Pathagomenan, cranberries, crowberies, mooseberries, &c," in *Voyages.*

[59] "My people" instead of "Mr. Leroux," in *Voyages.*

[60] From "and I can" to "winter" is omitted in *Voyages.*

way into a deep Bay to take the wind, when we came to hoist sail, we found we had forgotten our Mast at our Campment, landed and cut another, hoisted half sail which drove us on at a greate rate, at 12 the wind and swell augmented much, our underyard broke, but luckily our Mast Top resisted till we had time to fasten down the Yard with a Pole without lowering sail, took in much water, and had our Mast given way in all probability we should have filled and sunk, we went on with great Danger, being along a flat leeshore, not able to land till 3 oClock P.M. 2 men continually Bailing water which we took in on every side, doubled a Point which screened us from the wind and swell.[61] Camped for the Night, and to wait for our Indians, set nets, make a Yard and Mast, gummed our Canoe, visited our Nets, caught 6 small white *Fish*, and 2 pike, gathered plenty Cramberries and Crow Berries, Toward Night the weather became moderate.

MONDAY 24TH.—rose our Nets, caught 14 white Fish, 10 pike, and 2 Trout, embarked at 5 A.M. small Breezes from the Southward, hoisted sail, went on slowly as our Indians are behind, at 11 A.M. landed, to boil Kettle and dry our Nets that they may be ready for [us] to set to night, at one we again got underway, at 4 we perceived a Canoe with a sail and two small ones ahead, we soon came up with them, and found them Mr. Leroux, his Father in Law[62] and Family on a hunting Party, 26 Days since he left his House, It was his Intention to have gone as far as the Entrance of the River to leave a letter for me in case I should pass, he had seen no more Indians where I had left him, had made a Voyage to *Lac la Merde*,[63] where he found 18 small Canoes of the Slave Indians of whom he got 5 Pack chiefly Martins. there were 4 Beaver Indians among them, who had traded the greatest part of the above with the Slaves

---

[61] This sounds like present-day Slave Point. The north shore of Slave Lake to this point from the mouth of the north channel of the Mackenzie River is certainly not a very pleasant area to land on. Once around Slave Point the lake swings north, and the shore line is not quite so low.

[62] In *Voyages*, the "Father in Law" is not mentioned, and they had only been out twenty-five instead of twenty-six days.

[63] "Lac la Marte," in *Voyages*.

before his arrival, they informed him that their Relations had more Skins but that they were afraid to come with them, tho' they had heard French People were to come with goods to meet them, he gave them a pair of Trenches[64] each and other Trifles, sent them back to conduct their Friends to the Slave Lake, where he told them he was to remain next winter,[65] the Red Knives and Slaves were almost all gone to the *Carabouf* Country   he sent them Pawles, he has sent 16½ Packs to Athabsca, wrote for more goods which I had ordered him only to do in case he made 30 Packs, as I thot. it hardly worth while to establish a Post at such a distance witht. it produced that No., but it was the above reasons and his hopes of seeing them on the first Ice, which induced him to ask for foods, As soon as we landed my Men and Mr. Leroux's men set 3 nets, soon after caught 20 Fish of difft. sorts, about Dusk the English Chief arrived, came to my tent with a most pitiful look, that he had like to have got drowned following us, that his Brother[66] and other young men had a very narrow Escape. their Canoes broke at a distance from the shore, but as it was flat they made their Escape by his help, he left them crying to overtake me, that I might wait for them; that he is afraid they will not be able to mend their Canoe &c. &c. &c.

TUESDAY 25TH.—It was late this Morning before we got up gave some Rum to my Men last Night to divert themselves, visited our Nets, caught but few Fish, my Men live upon Leroux's Stores, at 11 A.M. the young Men arrived and repoached me for having left them so far behind, they had killed 2 Swans, and brought me one of them, the Wind southerly all Day, and too strong for us, are we at the Foot of a grand Traverse.[67] At noon I had an Observation

---

[64] "Ice chisels" instead of "Trenches," in *Voyages*.

[65] All, from this point to "set 3 nets," is missing in *Voyages*.

[66] No mention of "Brother," in *Voyages*.

[67] This last clause reads in *Voyages*, "we were at the foot of a grand traverse." The traverse appears to be the one across present-day Lonely Bay. There seems to be some question in his mind whether he is acually ready to make the traverse or whether he should follow the shore line a little further before cutting across Lonely Bay.

61° 29 North[68]   Can't visit our Nets. In the afternoon the Sky became over cast, lightening and loud Claps of Thunder the Wind veered round to the Westward and blew a Hurricane

WEDNESDAY 22D.[69]—Rained all last night and till 8 this morning, the Wind as yesterday, the Indians went ahunting, came back in the Evening with out killing anything. The English Chief missed an original[70]   In the afternoon heavy showers thunder &c.

THURSDAY 27TH.—Embarked before 4 A.M., hoisted sail at 9 A.M., landed to Cook Kettle and wait for Mr. Leroux and Indians, the former joined us at 11 o'Clock and we got under way, fine calm, at 4 P.M. Mr. Leroux broke his Canoe, landed to mend it,[71] a little Breeze from the southward, which we took the advantage of, at ½ past 5 P.M. camp'd set our Nets, no word of Mr. Leroux or the Indians, heard them Fire, The English Chief and People are quite exhausted with fatigue, he wanted to remain this morning to go to the Land of the Beaver Indians, and [said?] that he would be back to Athabasca in the course of the winter.

FRIDAY 28TH.—Blew hard all last Night and this morning, had much difficulty to go to our Nets, caught plenty white Fish, Trout &c. Toward the afternoon the wind augmented, 2 of the men who were gathering Berries saw 2 original, the Tracks of Buffaloes and Rein Deer, at Sun set we heard 2 shots, saw a fire on the opposite side of the Bay, we made a great fire that they might see where we are, after we all had gone to Bed heard the Report of a gun, soon after the English Chief made his appearance in a great flurry and quite wet, informed us that he believed the Frenchmen were drowned, and that his Brother and Companions had got their Canoe broke to pieces, lost their guns and the meat of a Rein Deer which they had killed this morning, that they were close by, asked a

---

68 This "Observation" suggests that they were about fifteen miles south of Lonely Bay, but if so there would not be a "grand traverse." There are numerous good fishing areas in this general locality today.

69 "26" in *Voyages*, which is obviously correct.

70 "Moose-deer" instead of "original," in *Voyages*.

71 The breaking and mending of Mr. Leroux's canoe is not mentioned in *Voyages*, nor is Leroux and his hunting party mentioned in the next few lines as they are in the Journal.

Frenchman to go and carry them as they were starving with cold however they and his women joined us, we gave them dry clothes to put on. It was so dark that it was impossible for us to go and look out for Mr. Leroux who they said had taken the Traverse along with them[72]

SATURDAY 29TH.—By the Break of Day I got up and went to see if I could learn anything of Mr. Leroux, before I came to where the Indians had landed, I saw a man coming along the Beach, it was an Indian who Mr. Leroux sent to tell me to send Men for the Meat of a Carrabouf, which he got from the Indian who had left him some time ago, he says their Canoe was full of water when they landed last night, Sent men for the Meat, my Indians went ahunting, at 11 oClk A.M. Mr. Leroux and his Indians arrived. The Hunters [returned?] without killing anything, They are determind. not to follow me any more, because they already ran so much risk and they are afraid of getting drowned, In the afternoon it became Calm, and I sent Mr. Leroux and all the Indians off and told them I should leave them all when Mr. Leroux had built, and that I would follow, tonight, Set our Nets.[73]

SUNDAY 30TH.—Embarked at 1 this morning, rose our Nets with a large Trout and 20 white Fish, at Sun rise passed Mr. Leroux and Indians where they had landed to rest a few hours,[74] about this time a smart aft Breeze arose which wafted us to Mr. Leroux's House,[75] by 2 P.M. It was late before the Indians arrived accordg. to promise I gave my Indians a good Equipment of Iron work, ammunition Tobacco &c. &c. as a recompence for

[72] The "Frenchmen" and "Mr. Leroux" and their making the traverse and perhaps being drowned are not mentioned in *Voyages*.

[73] The entry for "Saturday 29th," which in the Journal takes up nearly a page as seen above, is, in *Voyages*, covered in the following sentence: "I sent the Indians on a hunting party, but they returned without success; and they expressed their determination not to follow me any further, from their apprehension of being drowned."

[74] Passing Mr. Leroux and the Indians is not mentioned in *Voyages*.

[75] It is difficult to know where this house would be located exactly but very likely it was somewhere opposite present-day Whitebeach Point on the east side of the north arm of Great Slave Lake, somewhere near Latitude 62° 30'.

the misery they underwent along with me,[76] I ordered the English Chief to go to the Land of the Beaver Indians to bring them to Trade their Piltras with Mr. Leroux who I have [left?] here to winter, gave the latter what goods I had remaining, and promised to send him a few more Pieces, (should I not meet them after my arrival at Athabasca, as it will be the same Expense sending them now or next Spring, and by remaining here will be sure of what the Country is able to produce, The English chief is to be at Athabasca in the Month of March next with plenty of Beaver and Martins.

MONDAY 31ST.—I did not go to Bed all last Night, getting every thing in order to embark this morning. got a Bag of pounded meat and a little grease from Mr. Leroux suppose 80 lbs.   parted with them at 5 A.M. fine calm, at 10 A.M. we were obliged to land upon a small Island our Canoe taking in more water than common, we found that the Indian Children had shot an Arrow throw [through?] her under water mark. Cooked a Kettle of Fish here, lost 1½ Hour   at 12 the Wind rose from the S.E. this being the Direction we went in, impeded our March considerably. I had an Observation 62° 15 North, Camped at 7 oClock.[77]

SEPTEMBER 1789

TUESDAY 1ST. SEPTEMR.— We embarked at 5 A.M., fine calm weather, passed the Isle *la Cache*, at 12 could not perceive the land which we saw to the south when we passed here before   passed the Carrahouf Island at 5 P.M., see land to the S. and b W., which we think it [is?] the opposite of the lake extending a great distance, Camp'd at half past 6 P.M. Thunder and appearance of a change of Weather

[76] From this point *Voyages* sums up the remaining account of "Sunday 30" in two sentences: "I proposed to the English chief to proceed to the country of the Beaver Indians, and bring them to dispose of their peltries to M. Le Roux, whom I intended to leave there the ensuing winter. He had already engaged to be at Athabasca, in the month of March next, with plenty of furs."

[77] This reading suggests that they had made about half the necessary distance along the north arm toward present-day Gros Cap, which would put them in the vicinity of Yellowknife Bay.

THURSDAY 2D.[1]—Rained and blew hard the latter part of the last Night. the rain subsided at half pas[t] 6 A.M.[2] when we embarked in a Traverse of 12 Miles took a good deal of water, at 12 it became Calm, had an observation 61° 36 North, at 3 P.M. a slight Breeze from the Westward, it soon encreased, we hoisted sail and took a Traverse of 24 Miles for the point of the old Fort[3] where we arrived and landed for the night at 7 oClock. Our tak g this Traverse shortened our Road 3 Leagues, we did not expect to have got clear of the lake in such a situation

THURSDAY 3D.—Blew exceeding hard all Night, we embarked at 4 A.M. and [it] took us 3 hours to go 5 Miles without stopping, notwithstanding we were screened from the Swall [Swell?] by a large Bank, here we enter the River[4] where the Wind has no effect upon us, frequent showers today. Camp'd at 6 P.M.

FRIDAY 4TH.—Dark and Cloudy weather at 5 A.M. at 10 A.M.[5] we embarked, cleared up, see few Fowl. Camped at 7.

SATURDAY 5TH.—Cloudy weather, embarked at 5 A.M. at 8 began to rain very hard, put on shore and camp'd half an hour after. Detained all Day.

SUNDAY 6TH.—Rained all last night, a strong North wind, many numerous Flocks of wild fowl, pass to the Southward at 6 A.M.[6] the rain subsided a little, we embarked but it soon began again to pour down in Streams on us—an aft wind which we took the Ad-

[1] "Wednes. 2," in *Voyages*, which would seem correct.

[2] "Half past five," in *Voyages*.

[3] This could be present-day Grant Point where Grant had helped Leroux build a fort in 1786. (See footnote 20 of "June 1789.") However, the mileage given for "Thursday 3d" to get them into "the River" certainly must be off, or else the above "old Fort" must refer to some other place nearer the mouth of the Jean or the Slave River.

[4] The question is which river, the Jean or the Slave. Certainly "5 miles" won't get you to any sizeable river from Grant Point today. Could it possibly be that the Jean River had a different channel two hundred years ago, thus coming out nearer Grant Point than today, the older channel having been completely silted up during the past two centuries? One must remember that the Journal states only "6 miles" and *Voyages* "five miles" when Mackenzie first entered Great Slave Lake and was going to Grant's house on June 9, 1789. (See footnote 21, "June 1789.")

[5] "We embarked at five; but at ten it cleared up," in *Voyages*.

[6] *Voyages* uses "six in the afternoon," most likely a mistake.

vantage of at the Expense of a complete soaking   killed 7 geese today   Camped at ½ past 6 P.M.

MONDAY 7TH.—Embarked at half past 5 this morning, a hard wind, frequent showers of small Rain, at 3 oClk P.M. ran our Canoe upon a Stump, and before we could land she filled with Water, we took 2 Hours to repair her, we Camped at 7 oClk P.M.

TUESDAY 8TH.—Embarked at ½ past 4 A.M. a thick Mist till 9 A.M.   when it cleared away, fine weather   at 3 P.M. came to the first carrying place (Portage de Noyz)[7]   we camped at the upper end of it to dry our things, some of which are almost rotten

WEDNESDAY 9TH—at 5 A.M. the Canoe broke on the Mens shoulders in Portage De Chiligue,[8] the guide mended her while the others carried the Baggage, gummed our Canoe at Portage *le Montague*,[9] passed portages De Epinette De Barel De Embarass and De Casettle and camped at Riverieau Chum[10] at ½ past 4 P.M. men much fatigued   gummed our Canoe, made paddles to replace some broke coming up the Rapids, killed a Swan.

TUESDAY 10TH[11]—Embarked at ½ past 5 A.M., rained and blew hard last Night, this morning the former subsided and the latter augmented, Wind N.W.   at 7 A.M. hoisted sail. In the forenoon freqt Showers of Rain and Hail, in the Afternoon 2 Showers of Snow the wind very strong, at 6 oClock landed at a lodge of Crees,[12] 3 Men and 5 Women (children) they are on their return from War, one of them very sick. they parted with the rest of their Party in the Enemies Country thro Hunger (say 2 Men and their Families)[13]   after they had separated they met with a Family of the Enemy and destroyed them   they do not know what is become of

---

[7] *Portage de la Chétique*, in *Voyages*. Mackenzie is back in the area of present-day Fort Smith.

[8] *Portage de la Chétique*, in *Voyages*.

[9] *Portage de la Montagne*, in *Voyages*.

[10] The final four portages are not named in *Voyages*, and it says they "camped at the Dog River."

[11] "Thursday 10" in *Voyages*.

[12] "Knisteneaux," in *Voyages*.

[13] This parenthetical expression is left out of *Voyages*.

their Friends, they suppose they have returned from[14] the Peace River or starved. I gave Medicine to the Sick,[15] and a little ammunition to the healthy which they were much in need of, having lived by their Bows and Arrows this 6 Months, they have suffered very much.

FRIDAY 11TH.—Embarked at half past 4 A.M., froze hard last Night, cold weather throughout the Day, appearance of Snow, at 6 oClk P.M. landed for the Night at our Campment,[16] the Wind at N.E. and cold, at 8 oClock entered the lake of the Hills, at 10 the Wind veered to the Westward, and as strong as we could bear it with high Sail, which wafted us to Fort Chipewean by 3 oClk P.M. here we found Mr. McLeod with 5 Men busy building a new House 102 Days since we had left this place · /[17]

A few remarks to elucidate my tracks from Athabasca latitude 58. . 38 North and longitude 110½ West from Greenwich to the North Sea and western ocean, as delineated on Mr. Arrowsmith's Map.

Athabasca is 2750 Miles to the North and West of Montreal the distance from this to the North Sea in latitude 69¼ North and longitude about 135 West from Greenwich by the Slave lake and

[14] "To" instead of "from," in *Voyages.*

[15] Here *Voyages* uses an asterisk and adds a footnote (See pages 118 and 119 of *Voyages*) as follows: "This man had conceived an idea, that the people with whom he had been at war, had thrown medicine at him, which had caused his present complaint, and that he despaired of recovery. The natives are so superstitious, that this idea alone was sufficient to kill him. Of this weakness I took advantage; and assured him, that if he would never more go to war with such poor defenseless people, that I would cure him. To this proposition he readily consented, and on my giving him medicine, which consisted of Turlington's balsam, mixed in water, I declared, that it would lose its effect, if he was not sincere in the promise that he made me. In short, he actually recovered, was true to his engagements, and on all occasions manifested his gratitude to me."

[16] *Voyages* adds "of the third of June." This would be his camp on the Rocher River. It introduces the next paragraph as "Saturday 12" and starts, "The weather was cloudy and also very cold. At eight we embarked with a North-East wind, and entered the Lake of the Hills." It would seem that Mackenzie got in a hurry to finish and did not introduce Saturday. Counting June 3 as the first day, 102 days later would be the evening of September 12.

[17] Here *Voyages* stops. The next page starts Mackenzie on his next "Voyage." The Journal, however, has a blank page and then the three following pages are added.

Mac Kensies River is 1540 Miles. It was in the Summer of 1789 that I went this expedition in hopes of getting into Cook's River; tho' I was disappointed in this it proved without a doubt that there is not a North West passage below this latitude and I believe it will generally be allowed that no passage is practicable in a higher latitude the Sea being eternally covered with Ice.

In the prosecution of my journey to the western ocean in fall 1792, I took a fresh supply of provisions at Athabasca and passed on to the Unjegate, or Peace River, in which I went about 450 Miles against the current to the East of our settlements in this direction in latitude 56 & 9 North and longitude 117.3/4 west where I passed the winter. On the 9th May 1793 I took my departure from this the waters being then very high and strong, owing to the melting of the Snow. It took me thirty days to get to the source of the River, distance about 400 Miles, the tenth day I came to the rocky Mountains latitude 56 longitude 120 and ½ west which is more than half the above distance, the height of land only 750 paces broad is between two small lakes   we carried our Canoe and lading over the portage, went with the currant the river encreasing as we advanced til it lost itself in a larger branch which soon became a large river. After going down it about 420 Miles I learned from the Natives that as far as they had any knowledge of it, it went a Southern course. From their description and my own observations I concluded it to be a part or the whole of the River of the west. The distance to the Mouth of it would be too great for me to go and come back in the course of the season, particularly as my Canoe was so much damaged as to be unfit for use   therefore must lose time to make another, and that we had lost all our Bullets on which depended our safety and subsistance, we had some shot which we converted into balls but not enough   The natives gave me to understand that it was not far overland to the Sea and by their directions I returned some distance up the River   left my Canoe in latitude 53 North longitude 122.43 west. From this in 17 days I got to the sea coast; our course about west and distance 250 Miles, here I borrowed a wooden Canoe from the Indians &

went out about 20 leagues amongst the Islands this part of the coast is much interspersed with. My observations were 52.23 lat: and 128 and ¼ west long: answering nearly to Sr. Charles Middleton's Sound. The 22d. July I turned back by the way I went and arrived the 24th. Augst. at the place from which I had set out.

I have not the least doubt of this great River being navigable with Canoes and boats to its Mouth. I have mentioned above the cause of my not putting this to the proof. It abounds in Salmon and other fish, is well inhabited   they cloathe themselves in fur and skins and live by fishing and hunting.

Addenda

His Grace
  The Duke of Portland
    &c &c &c

MY LORD,

Mr McKenzie who has been employed by the associated Merchants of Montreal to make Discoveries in the Northwest parts of America, has sent me a short Narative of two Expeditions performed by him across this Continent. The great importance of the Trade carried on by those gentlemen may render it of consequence for His Majesty's Ministers to be more fully informed of Mr. McKenzie's Discoveries, and as he is about to proceed to England for the purpose of presenting a more particular account of them to your grace, I take this opportunity of recommending him to your notice

I am with great Respect and Esteem
  my Lord
    your Grace's
      Most Obedient
        humble Servant
          DORCHESTER[1]

To his Excellency Guy Lord Dorchester Governor General &
Commander in Chief of British America &c. &c.

MY LORD

It was my intention to have done myself the honor of waiting on your Lordship, but the state of my health deprives me of that

---

[1] Source: Public Record Office Reference, C. O. 42/401, duplicate no. 10. A super-

satisfaction: circumstances at present have made me determine
to go to England by way of the States, previous to which I think
it my duty to give your Lordship a short Sketch of two Expeditions
I have performed across this Continent; Humbly hoping it may
not be disagreeable to you.

The 3rd June 1789 I took my departure in a Bark Canoe, accompanied by five Canadians, & three Indians, from one of our
Settlements in the North West, Latitude 58° 33 North. Longititude
110½ West from Greenwich, I followed the course of the Waters
which had been reported by Mr. Pond to fall into Cooks River,
they led me to the Northern Ocean, in Latitude 69½ North, and
about 135 of West Longitude, by the 16th July the Sea was then
covered with ice at some distance from Sand, we saw a number of
white Porpoises, and observed there was a small Tide: Further,
it was needless for me to go, besides it would have been very dangerous to attempt to coast with such a slight Vessel as I had. Therefore we returned by the way we went.

Tho' this Expedition did not answer the intended purpose. It
proved that Mr Ponds assertion was nothing but conjecture, and
that a North West Passage is impracticable. Not having been furnished with proper Instruments to ascertain the Longitude in my
first Expedition. I made myself but little known during my residence in London the Winter 1791/92, but to prevent the like in-
conveniency I there purchased proper ones, in case I should make
a second attempt.

I left the Downs the 7th April 1792, and passed the following
Winter at one of our Western most Settlements in the Northwest,
on the Banks of a large River which the Natives name Unjegah,
in Latitude 56° 9 North, and Longitude 117° 40 West of Greenwich The 9th of May 1793 I proceeded in a Bark Canoe, ten of
us vize. an assistant, Six Canadians & two young Indians, to the
Source of this River: carried over the height of Land. (which is
only 700 yards broad) that separates those Waters, the one empties

script to the letter shows it was received March 7 and answered April 4. The following
letter from Mackenzie to Dorchester was enclosed.

into the Northern Ocean, and the other into the Western, in following the latter, they soon increased to the Size of a large River which I continued going down for a considerable distance   The rapidity of the Current, the Natives account of it convinced me that I could not go to its mouth & be back that season: from its course, and the information I received; I conclude it to be a part, If not the whole of the River of the West; this determined me to leave my Canoe in Latitude 53° North, & Longitude 122° 43 West and go over Land by a route the Natives frequent in going to the Western Ocean. to procure Iron & Trinkets for which they give Furs in Exchange to the Inhabitants of the Coasts, where I arrived the 18th of July, there being many Islands which prevented the view of the Main Ocean, I borrowed a Canoe from the Natives in order to go and get a sight of the open Sea, I went about sixty Miles yet was not gratified, the Inhabitants becoming troublesome, made it dangerous to proceed any further: The Latitude here I found to be 52° 23 North, and Longitude 128° 15 West, which Situation answers to Sir Chas. Middleton's Sound. The Inhabitants are well furnished with European Articles, few of them of any material use except the Iron, we could not understand those people therefore could not procure much intelligence from them. We came back the way we went, and arrived at the place of our departure the 24th of August

I am sorry I cannot give your Lordship a more particular account of this Expedition my Journal being as yet undigested.

> I have the honor to be
> > My Lord
> > > Your Lordship's
> > > > M. O. & v h. s.
> > > > > (Signed) ALEXR. MACKENZIE

MONTREAL 17th November 1794

Bibliography

MANUSCRIPTS AND DOCUMENTS

Cooper, P. F. "Antiquarianizing in the Mackenzie Delta," July 21, 1965. (I received a copy of this manuscript at the Inuvik Research Laboratory in Inuvik, N. W. T., in August, 1965).

Mackenzie, Alexander, "Journal to the North and Northwest Coast of America," 1789, British Museum, Stowe 793.

Mackenzie to Dorchester, Montreal, November 17, 1794, copy enclosed in Dorchester to Portland, No. 10, of November 20, 1794, C. O. 42, Vol. 101, Public Record Office of London.

Alexander Mackenzie Correspondence with Roderick Mackenzie, 1785–1816. Memorandum by Roderick Mackenzie. Public Archives of Canada, Ottawa, M. G. 19, d, Vol. 17.

Mackenzie to Messrs. McTauish Frobisher & Co., Montreal, New York, February 4 and 7, 1798. North West Company Correspondence, folios 277–280d, Hudson's Bay Record Society, Beaver House, London.

Six Legal Documents signed by Alexander Mackenzie, J. A. Grey-Index, 1796–1812, Superior Court, Department of Civil Status and of Archives, Montreal.

PUBLISHED MATERIALS

Bell, Robert. "Mackenzie District," Geological Survey of Canada, *Annual Report* (N.S.), No. XII (1900).

Bryce, George. *Mackenzie, Selkirk, Simpson.* London, Oxford University Press, 1926.

Burpee, Lawrence J. *The Search for the Western Sea: The Story of the Exploration of North Western America.* Toronto, The Musson Book Co., Ltd, 1908.

Campbell, Marjorie Elliott (Wilkins). *The North West Company*, New York, St. Martin's Press, 1957.

Camsell, Charles. "The Waterways of the Mackenzie River Basin," *Ottawa Naturalist*, Vol. XXVIII, No. 2 (May, 1914).

Camsell, Charles, and Wyatt Malcolm. "The Mackenzie River Basin," Canada Geological Survey, *Mus. Bull. No. 92*, Ottawa, Printer to the King's Most Excellent Majesty (1919).

Chambers, Ernest J. "The Great Mackenzie Basin," Reports of the select committees of the Senate sessions 1887 and 1888. Department of the Interior of Canada, 1910.

Crouse, Nellis. *La Vérendrye, Fur Trader and Explorer*. Ithaca, Cornell University Press, 1956.

Crouse, Nellis M. *The Search for the Northwest Passage*. New York, Columbia University Press, 1934.

Davidson, Gordon Charles. *The North West Company*. Berkeley, University of California Press, 1918.

Davies, R. A. *The Great Mackenzie in Word and Photograph*. Toronto, Ryerson Press, 1947.

De Sainville, Edouard. "Voyage à l'embouchure de la rivière Mackenzie (1889–1894)," *Bulletin de la Société de Géographie*, Tome XIX (1898).

Gates, Charles, ed. *Five Fur Traders of the Northwest*. Minneapolis, University of Minnesota Press, 1933.

Haworth, P. L. *Trailmakers of the Northwest*. New York, Harcourt, Brace & Co., 1921.

Hearne, Samuel. *A Journey from Prince of Wale's Fort in Hudson's Bay to the Northern Ocean*. Toronto, Champlain Society, 1911.

———. *A Journey from Prince of Wale's Fort, in Hudson's Bay, to the Northern Ocean, Undertaken by Order of the Hudson's Bay Company for the Discovery of Copper Mines, a Northwest Passage, etc., in the Years 1769, 1770, 1771, and 1772*. Dublin, 1796.

———, and Phillip Turnor. *Journals of Samuel Hearne and Phillip Turnor*. Toronto, Champlain Society, 1934.

Henry, Alexander (the Elder). *Travels and Adventures in Canada and the Indian Territories Between the Years 1760 and 1776*. New York, I. Riley, 1809.

Innis, Harold A. "The North West Company," *Canadian Historical Review*, Vol. VIII (1927).

————. *Peter Pond: Fur Trader and Adventurer*. Toronto, Irwin and Gordon, 1930.

Laut, A. C. *Pathfinders of the West*. Toronto, Ryerson Press, 1904.

McConnell, R. G. "Report on an Exploration in the Yukon and Mackenzie Basins, N. W. T.," Geological Survey of Canada, *Annual Report* (N.S.), No. IV (1891), Pt. D.

McDonald, Adrian. *Canadian Portraits*. Toronto, Ryerson Press, 1925.

McKay, J. Ross. "The MacKenzie Delta Area, N. W. T.," Geographical Branch, Mines and Technical Surveys, Mem. 8. Ottawa, Queen's Printer, 1963.

Mackenzie, Alexander. *Voyages from Montreal, on the River St. Laurence, through the Continent of North America, to the Frozen and Pacific Oceans; in the Years 1789 and 1793. With a Preliminary Account of the Rise, Progress, and Present State of the Fur Trade of that Country*. London, Cadell and Davis, 1801.

Manning, Clarence A. *Russian Influence on Early America*. New York, Library Publications, 1953.

Masson, Louis R. *Les Bourgeois de la Compagnie du Nord-ouest*. 2 vols. Quebec, Cote, 1889.

Montgomery, Franz. "Alexander Mackenzie's Literary Assistants," *Canadian Historical Review*, Vol. XVIII (1937).

Payette, B. C. *The Northwest*. Montreal, privately printed for Payette Radio Limited, 1964.

Petitot, Émile. "Géographie de l'Athabaskaw-Mackenzie et des grands lacs du bassin arctique," *Bulletin de la Société de la Géographie*, Sixième Série, Tome 10 (Paris, 1875).

Rich, E. E. *The History of the Hudson's Bay Company, 1670–1870*, 2 vols. London, The Hudson's Bay Record Society, 1958.

Roberts, Leslie. *The Mackenzie*. New York, Rinehart & Co., 1949.

Sage, Walter N. "Sir Alexander Mackenzie and His Influence on the History of the North West." *Bulletin* of the Departments of

Historical, Political, and Economic Science. Queens University, *No. 43* (1922).

Sheppe, Walter, ed. *First Man West: Alexander Mackenzie's Journal of His Voyage to the Pacific Coast of Canada in 1793.* Berkeley, University of California Press, 1962.

Vail, Philip. *The Magnificent Adventures of Mackenzie.* New York, Dodd, Mead & Co., 1964.

Wade, Mark S. *Mackenzie of Canada.* London, Blackwood, 1927.

Wagner, Henry. *Peter Pond: Fur Trader & Explorer.* New Haven, Yale University Press, 1955.

Wallace, W. Stewart, ed. *Documents Relating to the North West Company.* Toronto, Champlain Society, 1934.

Woollacott, Arthur P. *Mackenzie and his Voyageurs by Canoe to the Arctic and the Pacific, 1789–1793.* London, J. M. Dent & Sons Ltd., 1927.

Wrong, Hume. *Sir Alexander Mackenzie.* Toronto, Macmillan Co., 1927.

Index

Alberta: 7
Arbuckle, Franklin, R.C.A.: 7n.
Arlington, Earl of: 5
Arctic Circle: 23
Arctic Ocean: 3, 18, 23
Arctic Watershed: 10–11
Arrowsmith's map: 116
Athabasca: 3, 6, 9, 11–15, 25, 32, 39, 66, 79, 95, 107, 110, 111, 113, 116
Athabasca Indians: 9–10
Athabasca, Lake: 5, 7–8, 10–11, 15
Athabasca River: 11

Beads: 18, 50, 64, 80, 82, 84, 86, 88, 90–92
Bear Lake: 8
Bears: 56, 69, 72, 82
Beaulieu (French-Indian family): 13
Beaver: 5, 17, 28–30, 32, 36, 38–39, 47, 49, 55, 59, 86, 90, 96, 100, 103, 105
Beaver Indians: 36, 44, 101, 107, 109, 111
Beaver Lake: 10–11
Belahoulay Cown (white men's fort): 88
Belan howlay Tock (white men's lake): 18, 66, 82, 86
Berries: 31, 39, 78, 105, 108
Birds: 30–31, 43, 71–72, 79, 105
Bow & Arrow: 45, 61, 82, 84, 116
British Museum: 4
Buffaloes: 30, 44, 56, 82, 89, 91, 106, 111

Canadian fur houses: 12
Canoes: 23, 25–27, 30, 38, 55, 57, 70, 72–74, 75–76, 82, 98, 103; gumming of, 25, 92, 107, 115
Caribou (Careboeuff): 97, 110, 112

Carr, George: 5
Charles II: 5–6
Chipewyan Indians: 7–8, 10, 17, 38, 55, 83
Coppermine River: 8
Churchill (Fort Prince of Wales): 7–8, 12
Churchill River: 10–11
Churchill River District: 14
Coal: 96
Cocking, Mathew: 9
Combe, William: 4, 24
Cook's River: 88, 117
Copper: 8, 17, 83
Chipewyan Language: 50
Cree Indians: 6, 19, 22, 40, 46, 48, 107, 115
Cumberland House: 9–11

Delta area of Mackenzie River: 22, 65–79
Dogs: 80, 91, 99, 101, 104
Dogrib Indians: 7, 18, 50–55, 86
Dog River: 26, 115

Edinburgh: 3
England: 5
"English Chief" (Chipewyan Indian leader and interpreter): 15, 38, 40, 42–43, 50–51, 61, 70–72, 78, 80–81, 83–84, 86, 91–92, 94–96, 100–106, 110–11, 113; quarrel with, 102–104
Eskimos (Eskmeaux): 17–18, 22, 61, 63–64, 66–79, 84; dishes, 18, 70, 75; sledges, 18, 70, 75–76; fishery, 67–68; huts, 68–70; tools, 69–70; fence, 77; winter quarters, 77; lakes, 87; *see also* canoes

Fish: 18, 30–34, 40, 57, 62, 72, 109; drying of, 81, 86; roe, 81
Fisheries: 40, 108
Flint: 17, 50, 82
Fort, traders: 9
Fort, *Unalaschka*: 88
Fort Chepwean (Chipewyan): 15, 25, 116
Fort Good Hope: 17–18, 58n.

Fort Norman: 50n.
Fort Providence: 13, 19
Fort Resolution: 13
Fort York: 9–10, 12
Foxes: 63, 69, 74, 82, 86, 98
French: 5, 6, 12, 19, 22, 38, 87, 92, 96, 104, 110, 111–12
French-Canadian: 5
French-Indian: 13
Frobisher, Joseph: 9–10, 12
Frobisher, Thomas: 9–10, 12
Fur trade: 5–6, 50–51; *see also* beaver and names of companies

Gifts: 57–58, 60
Grand Portage (Indian village): 14
Grant, Cuthbert: 13n., 28, 30
Great Bear Lake: 55, 90, 95
Great Bear River: 55, 90
Great Lakes: 5–6
Great Slave Lake: 6, 8, 10, 13, 15–16, 19, 22–23, 25, 29–43, 83, 101, 108–14, 116
Great Western River: 86, 88–90, 95
Greenwich, England: 116
Gregory, McLeod and Company: 12–14
Grenville, George (first Marquis of Buckingham): 4
Groseilliers, Medard Chouart, sieur des Groseilliers: 5
Grover, William: 7

Hair Indians: 59, 86
Hares: 58, 82, 85, 100
Hearne, Samuel: 8–9, 12–13, 16
Henry, Alexander Henry the elder: 9
Henry, Alexander the younger: 10
Henday, Anthony: 6
Horn Mountains: 44, 106
Hudson's Bay: 5–6
Hudson's Bay Company: 6–7, 9–12
Hudson's Bay Record Society: 7–8
Hudson's House: 12

Ice: 3, 26; on Great Slave Lake, 29–36, 40–42; on Mackenzie River, 46, 82, 94; on the delta, 70–71, 73
Independents: *see* Pedlars
Indians: clothing, 16, 51–52, 61–62; dishes, 16, 53–54, 103; jewelry, 16, 52; arms, 17, 54, 103; dance, 51, 90; huts, 81, 85–86, 92; roads, 96, 98–99; children, 113
Île à la Crosse: 10
Isham, Charles: 10
Isle de Carribo: 35, 113
Isle la Cach: 35, 113
Iron: 17–20, 46, 55, 61, 81–82, 86, 90, 95, 112

Jacobs, Ferdinand: 7, 9

Knight, James: 6

Lac la Merde: 109
Lac la Ronge: 12
Lake of the Hills: 116
La Pérouse (French sailor and explorer): 12
Leroux, Laurent (trader for Northwest Fur Company): 15–16, 25, 29–31, 34–36, 38–40, 108–113; house of, 112
Liard River: 19, 46, 104
Little Chicago: 17
London, England: 3, 5
Louisiana Purchase: 3

Macbeath, George: 9
Mackenzie, Alexander: 3–5, 7, 11, 15–19, 22–23; Journal, 3, 4–5, 16–17, 22–24
Mackenzie River: 5–8, 22–23, 38, 42–108, 117; basin of, 6, 8; north channel of, 16, 23, 43–44
Mackenzie, Roderick: 4n., 14–15, 39
McLeod: 39, 116
McTavish, Simon: 12
Marten, Humphrey: 10
Martin (pelts): 17, 55, 82, 86, 103, 109
Matonabbee: 8

Mer d' Ouest: 72
Mirde Dours: 107
Mississippi River: 5
Montreal, Canada: 9, 14, 116
Moose: 30, 41, 44, 70, 91, 96, 108, 111

New England: 5
Natural resources: 47, 83, 95, 96, 104; *see also* iron
Northern Ocean: 66
North Pacific Ocean: 15
North Sea (on Arrowsmith's map): 116
North West Fur Company: 3, 6, 10–14, 25
Northwest passage: 3, 5, 15, 117
Norton, Moses: 8
Noxta Sound: 88

"Old Establishment": 11, 15
Old Fort Chipewyan: 3, 23

Pacific Ocean: 15
Pangman, Peter: 13
Patterson, Charles: 9
Peace River: 10, 25, 116, 117
"Pedlars" (non-Company traders): 7, 9–10, 11, 12
Pemican: 35, 46, 77, 101
Physical features: 6, 8, 16, 42, 69–70, 76–78, 100, 109, 117
Pine Island Lake: 9
Plants, indigenous: 34, 65, 78, 91
Point Du Roch: 28
Pond, Peter: 9–15
Portage De Barel: 115
Portage De Casettle: 115
Portage De Chiligue: 115
Portage, d Embarass: 27, 115
Portage De Epinette: 115
Portage, Mountain: 27, 115
Portage, Pelican: 27
Prairies: 6

Presents: *see* gifts
Primeau, Louis: 10
Prison: 3
Provisions: 73, 82–83, 94, 106
Punctuation: 4

Quarreller Indians (*Diguthe Dinees*): 17–18, 64, 84–85

Radisson, Pierre Esprit: 5–6
Ramparts: 17
Rapids: 26–29, 46, 48, 56, 84, 87, 92, 94, 107, 115
Red Knife Indians: 17, 19, 36, 55, 105, 110
Reindeer: 17, 30, 33, 35, 41, 58–59, 75, 77–78, 82, 84, 87, 96, 98, 111
Red Deer River: 7
Red River: 9
River of the west: 117
Rocky Mountains: 6, **7, 117**
Ross, John: 14
Rum: 38, 104, 110

Saskatchewan River: 6–7, 9, 12
Slave Indians: 7–8, 36, 50–55, 109
Slave River: 6, 8, 10, 27, 31, 114
Smallpox: 12
Snow: 70, 96, 115, 117
Stewart, William: 6
Storms: 85, 93, 111
Sturgeon Lake: 9
Superior, Lake: 9
Sutherland (Highland trader): 15

Tides: 74–75
Tow line: 79, 83, 93
Trees: 26, 48, 65, 83, 99, 105

Vérendrye, Pierre Gaultier de Varennes, sieur de la Vérendrye: 6, 7

Waden, Jean Étienne: 12

Weather: 85, 93, 111
Western Ocean (on Arrowsmith's map): 116–17
Whales: 69, 73, 75
Whale Island: 3
Winter Road River: 87
Wolves: 98, 101
Wrigley: 48n.

Yellowknife Bay: 36n.
York Factory: 6
Yukon River: 86n.

The type face chosen for EXPLORING THE NORTHWEST TERRITORY is Linotype Old Style No. 7, a modernized old style based upon a face cut by the Bruce Foundry in the early 1870's. Old Style No. 7 is noted for its splendid, even color and uncommon legibility. The paper upon which the book is printed bears the watermark of the University of Oklahoma Press and has an effective life of at least three hundred years.